FORGOTTEN MEMORIES

FROM A FORGOTTEN BLITZ

By Neil Anderson

ISBN 978-1-908431-11-0

Every effort has been made to trace the copyright holders of photographs in this book but one or two were unreachable. We would be grateful if the photographers concerned would contact us.

Published by ACM Retro Ltd,
The Grange,
Church Street,
Dronfield,
Sheffield S18 1QB.

Visit ACM Retro at:
www.acmretro.com

A catalogue record for this book is available from the British Library.

FORGOTTEN MEMORIES

FROM A FORGOTTEN BLITZ

By Neil Anderson

A vision of hell - Sheffield city centre on December 12/13 1940

HALLAM MOORS
REDMIRES RESERVOIRS
HATHERSAGE
BURBAGE MOOR
HATHERSAGE MOOR
WESTERN EXTENSION
BEELEY WOOD
Recreation Ground
Birley Carr
WADSLEY BRIDGE
R. Don
LONGLEY
Longley Park
Southey Green
WADSLEY
Bower Plantation
Wisewood
HILLSBOROUGH
HILLSBOROUGH PARK
OWLERTON
Norwood
Upper Crabtree
R. Loxley
Malin Br
Stannington Wood
Woodland View
Lower Walkley
Recreation Grd.
NEEPSEND
Parkwood Springs
PITSMOOR
Burngreave Cemetery
Knowle Top
WALKLEY
Walkley Bank
Liberty
Stannington
Bole Hill Rec. Grd.
Steel Bank
CROOKESMOOR
CROOKES
Rails
R. Rivelin
Crosspool
Lydgate
Blackbrook Wood
Tapton Hill
Broomhill
SANDYGATE
Hallam Head
Endcliffe Edge
Gorsick Hill
RANMOOR
Nether Green
Bingham Park
General Cemetery
HIGHFIELD
Recreation Grd.
FULWOOD
GREYSTONES
BRINCLIFFE
Brincliffe Tower
HEELEY
Whiteley Wood
Hill Top
ECCLESALL
MEERSBROOK
MEERSBROOK PARK
Bents Green
Ringinglow
Playing Fields
Bole Hill Plantation
Rough Standhills
Parkhead
MILLHOUSES
R. Sheaf
MILLHOUSES & ECCLESALL
Whirlow
WOODSEATS
University Athletic Grounds
ECCLESALL WOOD
Cemetery
Bolehill
GRAVES PARK
Abbeydale
Oakwood
BEAUCHIEF
Norton
NORTON PARK
Beauchief
Parkbank Wood
Little Norton
Couseway Head

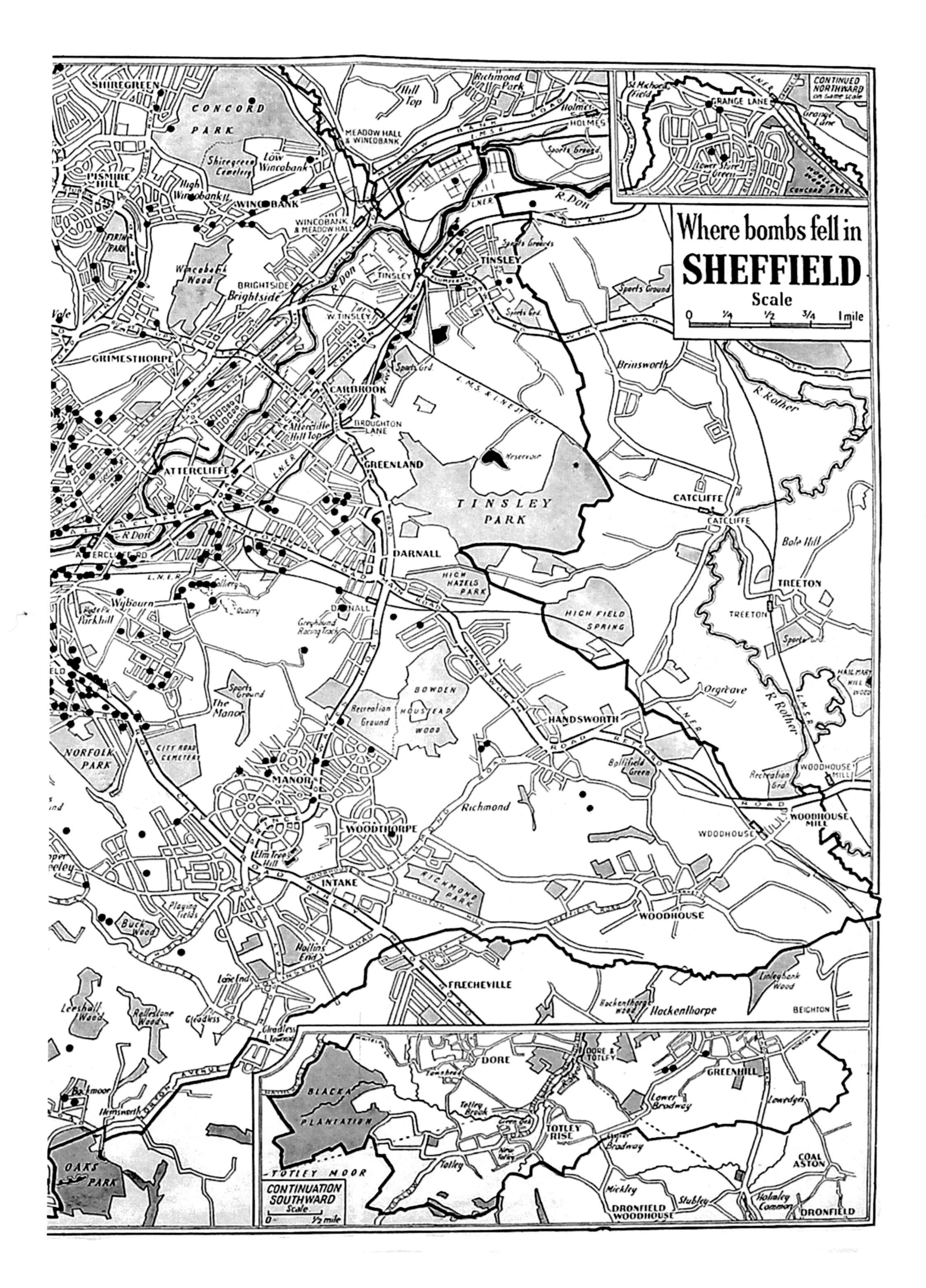

Where bombs fell in
SHEFFIELD
Scale
0
1/4
1/2
3/4
1 mile
CONTINUED NORTHWARD on same scale
CONTINUATION SOUTHWARD

'Help the Housewife' was the Girl Guides' slogan - here were two hanging out the washing for a war worker. Around 3,000 guides were providing this type of assistance.

CONTENTS

Sheffield The Forgotten Blitz presenter Terry Deary unveils the first Sheffield Blitz Heritage Trail plaque outside Atkinsons on The Moor

The Atkinsons plaque

Introduction

Nothing could have prepared me for the incredible reaction to *Sheffield's Date With Hitler* book when it was first published in 2010.

I was nervous about tackling a subject that scarred an entire generation (my family included); left over 2,000 people dead or injured and still posed so many unanswered questions about the real reason for the attacks and the seemingly indiscriminate way, in many cases, the bombs were dropped.

Scores of largely forgotten heroes showed their true mettle on the streets of Sheffield over those two hellish nights in December 1940.

No fewer than Six George Medals were awarded for bravery.

The way the city coped with the attacks and the aftermath was held up as an example to the entire country by Prime Minister Winston Churchill.

Two years since *Sheffield's Date With Hitler* and I've lost track of the amounts of talks, presentations and interviews I've done on the Sheffield Blitz.

Seeing the book form the basis of BBC1 documentary, *Sheffield The Forgotten Blitz*, was an amazing feeling.

But the more I learnt about the subject, the more I was saddened by the lack of widespread and lasting ways to mark the sacrifices made by the city in World War Two.

It seems incredible that there is no permanent exhibition in the city to mark the attacks.

Younger generations have grown up with a city centre made up of faceless, sixties concrete buildings. Many have no idea so much of Sheffield city centre's beautiful heritage was razed to the ground by the Luftwaffe in December 1940.

Sheffield Blitz Memorial Fund was set up in November 2011 to change that situation.

Our first aim is the creation of a Sheffield Blitz Memorial Trail with markers on key sites around the city centre.

The campaign has won cross-party support at Sheffield Town Hall and high-profile benefactors including Sheffield-born nightclub impresario Peter Stringfellow and Terry Deary, creator of the multi-million selling *Horrible Histories* series.

Boy Scouts were essential to the war effort in Sheffield

This book is the result of spending hours interviewing scores of Sheffield Blitz survivors who were in the thick of the carnage on December 12 and December 15, 1940.

Though the events took place 72 years ago, the memories are as fresh and as shocking as the day they happened.

94-year-old Doug Lightning is reputed to be the last remaining member of the Sheffield Police Fire Brigade that fought the Blitz fires, saw colleagues and civilians die in front of his eyes and saw his beloved city go up in flames; Maurice Wilkinson still hangs on to the remains of the incendiary bomb that came through the roof of his Nether Edge home, the same house he lives in today and Shirley Smith still visits the house she lived in as a child that sits on the edge of Devonshire Green, a once vibrant working class city centre community that was virtually bombed out of existence on December 12, 1940.

She was one of the hundreds of people who

spent Christmas 1940 in High Storrs Rest Centre.

97-year-old Nellie Bennett can still remember the end of the war that was meant to be the end of all wars, Armistice Day in Sheffield in 1918; the grief of her Broomgrove Nursing Home colleague Douglas Oldfield has remained with him to this day, his sister lost her entire family when their city centre home was hit in December 1940. Douglas's family tried to look after her but she could never get over the loss, she lived out her tormented days in Middlewood Hospital.

Joyce Spurr met the bombed out victims as they arrived at the Central Library on Surrey Street within hours of the last bomb dropping on Friday, December 13. It was the designated information centre and organised with military precision to help people rebuild their lives as quickly and efficiently as possible.

Forgotten Memories From A Forgotten Blitz is a collection of incredible memories picked for their bravery, tenacity and the power of the human spirit. They were ordinary people caught up in extraordinary times; we hope we'd act as they did if the country ever faced such terror again. They hope nobody would have to go through what they did.

All profits from this book will go to the Sheffield Blitz Memorial Fund (www.sheffieldblitz.co.uk).

Neil Anderson.

VE Day celebrations in Sheffield

CHAPTER ONE
'God help us all' - war is declared

Few people were in any doubt war was coming. Hitler had made little secret of his intent since the day he came to power in 1933.

British Prime Minister Neville Chamberlain's appeasement policy had done everything possible to stave off the inevitable and, many would argue, allowed Germany to grow far stronger as a result.

The Nazi invasion of Poland that started on September 1, 1939, signalled time running out for appeasement and the final countdown to a war that would go on to claim the lives of over fifty million people.

Britain ground to a halt at just after 11am on Sunday, September 3, as the nation crowded round the radio to hear their Prime Minister solemnly announce the gravest news imaginable:

"I am speaking to you from the Cabinet Room at 10 Downing Street.

"This morning the British Ambassador in Berlin handed the German Government a final note stating that, unless we hear from them by 11 o'clock that they were prepared at once to withdraw their troops from Poland, a state of war would exist between us. I have to tell you now that no such undertaking has been received, and that consequently this country is at war with Germany.

"You can imagine what a bitter blow it is to me that all my long struggle to win peace has failed.

"Yet I cannot believe that there is anything more or anything different that I could have done and that would have been more successful.

"Up to the very last it would have been quite possible to have arranged a peaceful and honourable settlement between Germany and Poland, but Hitler would not have it. He had evidently made up his mind to attack Poland, whatever happened, and although he now says he put forward reasonable proposals which were rejected by the Poles, that is not a true statement.

"The proposals were never shown to the Poles, nor to us, and though they were announced in a German broadcast on Thursday night, Hitler did not wait to hear.

"His action shows convincingly that there is no chance of expecting that this man will ever give up his practice of using force to gain his will. He can only be stopped by force.

Neville Chamberlain returns from Munich with his famous 'Peace In Our Time' paper - it was in tatters within months

"We and France are today, in fulfilment of our obligations, going to the aid of Poland, who is so bravely resisting this wicked and unprovoked attack upon her people. We have a clear conscience - we have done all that any country could do to establish peace.

"The situation in which no word given by Germany's ruler could be trusted, and no people or country could feel itself safe, has become intolerable. And now that we have resolved to finish it I know that you will play your part with calmness and courage.

"At such a moment as this the assurances of support which we have received from the empire are a source of profound encouragement to us.

"When I have finished speaking, certain detailed announcements will be made on behalf of the government. Give these your closest attention. The government have made plans under which it will be possible to carry on work of the nation in the days of stress and strain that may be ahead...

"Now may God bless you all. May he defend the right. For it is evil things that we shall be fighting against - brute force, bad faith, injustice, oppression and persecution - and against them I am certain that right will prevail."

Many people in Sheffield simply broke down at the news. The reaction of Marlene Dale's (nee Cavell) mum and grandma was typical.

She said: "I can still remember mum and grandma listening to Chamberlain announce: 'We are now at war with Germany'. They were stood there hugging one another and crying.

"I had a dad in the RAF who was in Balloon Command stationed on Wincobank Hill. We used to go up every Sunday to see him and my mum used to cook them their Sunday dinner.

"We lived on Hartley Brook Road on Shiregreen when the bombs fell. I was frightened to death. We had a budgie that we couldn't get in his cage. He flew into the fire and burned his tail. He died.

"We had a three storey house and we'd had one part of the basement reinforced. We had bunks in there. They'd loosened some bricks so we'd an escape hatch if necessary. We laid on our bunks, terrified.

"We didn't have an immediate devastation on our road but the nearby Flower estate copped it terrible. My mum worked at Capital Cinema on Barnsley Road as a cleaner and usherette. We used to have to sit on the back row when she was working so we saw every film going, suitable or not.

"That became a rest centre for all the people that had been bombed out. I can still see them sat in the cinema seats with their bundles. I remember helping dish cups of tea out. They ended up bringing all the staff in to help.

"I should have started at Hartley Brook Road Primary school in the September as war broke out but it was taken over as an ARP station. So Home Service was announced which provided classes in peoples' houses.

"My starting class was to be on our road at the house of a friend I used to play with. They were doing it in her spare bedroom. I can still remember standing crying on the landing because I didn't want to go."

Gas mask drills were commonplace in Sheffield months before war finally broke out

Ack-ack guns on Wadsley Common

Lillian Clay said: "World War Two broke out when I was eighteen. I can always remember when they announced it on the radio. I was at my mum's in Hillsborough. She said: 'God help us all'.

"I remember we had to carry our gasmasks about everywhere. I had a gas-cot for my baby.

"My dad said after the first night of the Blitz: 'Don't go into town whatever you do. It's terrible. It's razed to the ground.' I remember trams were on fire, shops were on fire and everything.

"We were in an Anderson Shelter in Hillsborough.

"We were in the one belonging to the lady next door as there was plenty of room in hers. It was dome-like in shape. You went in and down some stairs and sat on slats. It was damp. You had to wait in there until the all clear went. I could hear our Ack-ack guns on Wadsley Common. You could hear the German planes as they were a different noise to ours.

"The nearest a bomb got to us was a long road that runs down the side of Hillsborough Park - every house was razed to the ground by a landmine."

Home Guard drills in Sheffield and Rotherham

First aid exercises

ARP volunteers in Sheffield

Hitler and his Nazi henchmen

Re-enacting the Munich Putsch of 1923 in a bid to glorify an event that had been a total disaster

Debris and burnt out trams on Snig Hill

Sir Oswald Mosley with his chief organisers, prior to meeting of the British Union of Facists at the City Hall in Sheffield

CHAPTER TWO
Last customer at Sheffield's oldest hostelry

What was left of the King's Head Hotel

Maurice Wilkinson was one of the final customers at the historic King's Head Hotel on Change Alley. It was lucky he left when he did. The hotel was one of many hostelries lost that night. His luck held out right through the night despite the family home being hit.

His sharp-thinking ensured he's still living in the same house today, and still holds what remains of the incendiary bomb that came through the roof and set fire to the attic. After the war he went on to a glittering career as a ballet dancer.

Maurice Wilkinson said: "The war was coming, we were rationed and mother was busy with a huge knitting circle - knitting for the navy. She was glad of me to cook the lunch and things like that - I always liked cooking.

"I was nineteen and living at home, not sure if I wanted to use ballet or elocution for my career and then along came the war. I remember being in our church, one that has now fallen down, and the vicar going up into the pulpit and saying: 'Ladies and gentlemen, it's my painful duty to tell you we're now at war with Germany'.

"Well not much happened for a bit but then, in late 1940, things hotted up.

"I was friendly with a girl in dancing school and I'd been due to take her for a dance one Thursday night.

"I'd got a very funny feeling about that night. I remember saying to my mother in the day that 'I really wish I wasn't going to that dance tonight'. 'Shall I pretend I'm poorly?', I said. She said: 'No, that would make you a liar'.

"When I set off driving to Orgreave to collect her I decided to stop off in the city centre and have a little tonic to help buck my spirits up.

"So I went to the King's Head Hotel on Change Alley which, later on that night, received a direct hit.

"I remember the whole town seemed ever so quiet and I was the only one in the bar.

"Whilst I was in, the barmaid started turning off all the lights and I said: 'What are you doing'? Well she'd had the warning that something was going to happen. She said 'the purple's on and I've a feeling we're going to get the red'.

"Well I thought 'that's a good excuse, now I can go home and I don't have to go to the dance'!

"I started driving back home. It was foggy and I was following a tram up Abbeydale Road. When I turned up Chippinghouse Road there was a great incandescent pile on the footpath and I could hear aircraft up above. It was an incendiary bomb. They were dropped first in order to get property alight and guide the way for the rest of the raid.

"I thought 'I'm going to be bombed'. I drove the rest of the way home like hell for leather. I'd lost a headlamp on the way home and my father was stood waiting for me.

"We didn't have an air raid shelter - my father didn't build one, he wasn't a very organised man.

"The only refinement we had was carpet on the cellar floor, gas and electric light and three beds.

"Some people had absolutely gorgeous shelters.

"The fact we were in the cellar actually saved the house in the end. We were in the cellar when the bombs were falling. We had two dogs and a cat and a canary with us.

"My mother, father and I sat on a bed and waited to be bombed. We sat very close - we thought our time is very close. You would hear a very shrill whistle and then, about two seconds later, you would hear the explosion. We thought we'd be dead in half an hour - we thought our time is now up.

Many spent time making their air raid shelter an attractive feature of their garden

"I was very devoted to my parents, I loved them dearly and I would have much preferred for us all to have been killed rather than just one of us.

"Then my dad smelled smoke and we went up into the house to see what was happening and an incendiary bomb had come through the roof and the attic was well alight.

"The heat of the fire was so bad I couldn't get near it, so I had to go up and down stairs with bowls of water and throw them through the rails of the banister on to the fire

"For two hours I kept at it until the fire finally went out.

"We went back to the cellar which was wet through by now with all the water from the fire.

"The next morning we came upstairs and the police came round to tell us that there were 60 unexploded bombs in the street.

"An old neighbour came to the door in floods of tears. I hate to see a man cry. He had lost everything.

"He and his family were warm and snug in their air raid shelter while their house burned to the ground.

"They didn't know until the morning."

'People realised they had to work together to get through it'

Jean Grindle said: "We had everything in our Anderson Shelter. We thought it was all right. There was a funny smell after the Blitz, all smoky and horrid. We had to stay in our shelter for a few days after the bombing.

"My dad would say: 'Shhhhh listen' and we'd hear a 'swish, bang' as the bombs fell. We left the shelter in the morning and everything was in bits. Good actually came out of the bad as everyone helped everyone else.

"My dad would help the old ladies. I think we became better people. We'd share things, nobody would be left out. I often think how lucky I've been to live amongst that generation - it taught me a lot. I thought, if we can get through that we can get through anything. It showed how bad things could really get. People realised they had to work together to get through it. The atmosphere changed, I remember knitting a lot for people - we all did something."

Total desolation in Vicar Lane

Shops in High Street

What was left of the Three Horse Shoes Hotel and Tivoli Cinema

CHAPTER THREE
Roy survives a direct hit

It's a miracle Roy Shenton is here to tell his story his story at all. The public air raid shelter he was in took a direct hit. He was thirteen and a half when war broke out. He never had another day at school. His experience wasn't uncommon as houses became makeshift classrooms up and down the city for the duration of the conflict.

Roy Shenton said: "Before war broke out I went to Sharrow Lane School but that was evacuated when the war started. My education was fitted into two afternoons a week at Mrs Cookson's house on South View Road. We never knew what subject we were going to have or what teacher we were going to have.

"I had no qualifications when I finished.

"People say we were the deprived teenagers. I was nineteen when the war ended and thirteen when it broke out. The blackout came on and there was no entertainment, nowhere to go and nothing to do.

"We used to either go to the Heeley Coliseum, Abbeydale Picture Palace or the Heeley Palace. I remember it was six pence upstairs and four pence downstairs.

"On the screen, normally after the picture had started, you'd suddenly get 'purple warning' which meant there were squadrons heading towards Sheffield. They could well end up going to Liverpool or somewhere further north. The 'purple warning' meant the film would continue but it acted as an advance warning for the audience. My father told me: 'If a purple warning comes on you leave the building immediately and you come home'. Even in those times we soon realised it wasn't a very

A mass of twisted steel - all that was left of C&A Modes on High Street

profitable mode of entertainment as we were losing four pence every time we went and had to leave early.

"I ended up working as an apprentice with my father, doing 40 hours a week. I didn't like it. I knew I wasn't going to end up working in the steelworks for the rest of my life. My father was work mad.

"He worked alternate shifts, 12 hours a day. He never did anything in the house like decorating or gardening.

"We lived at Sherrington Road in Highfields area but my mother always wanted to get out of our two up, two down house where me and my two older brothers shared a bedroom. She looked round herself and found a bay windowed house opposite Sharrow Lane School in Vincent Road. I had a day off school to help her to move.

"My father went out of the house at Sherrington Road in the morning and at night was making enquiries either side of where we lived to ask 'where have the new people come?' He had never, ever, visited the house we were moving into.

"My life was going to work, listening to the wireless, reading a book and going to bed.

"I came home on the first night of the Blitz with no indication of what sort of a night it was going to be. My father got home about six and he said: 'There seems to be an awful lot of activity going on - searchlights and all sorts like that'.

"He'd hardly got in the house and the sirens went.

"Now there was a shelter under the school and the entrance was within 50 yards of where we lived.

"We crossed the road and went into their reinforced shelter. There were seats on either side. We'd been in before when the sirens had gone. We'd regularly be home within a few minutes if nothing happened.

"That night people were saying: 'This could be the night for us'. Coventry, Liverpool and Birmingham were all catching it. It wasn't long before we could hear this banging and that went on from about half past seven until about two o'clock in the morning.

"The school got a direct hit with a bomb. Bricks and everything came down on our shelter. People were crying and there was dust flying about everywhere and my brother had blood pouring down his face.

"There were a few people injured but nothing serious. My brother got cut on his head and he had to be taken by one of the wardens up to the Royal Hospital on West Street.

"We caught it very badly in our part of town.

"The all clear went and we went outside. The road was covered with fragments of shells and bricks.

"Nobody had any windows left as far as you could see. We went back into our house and one of the ceilings was down and the windows blown in.

"My mother took charge and we started clearing

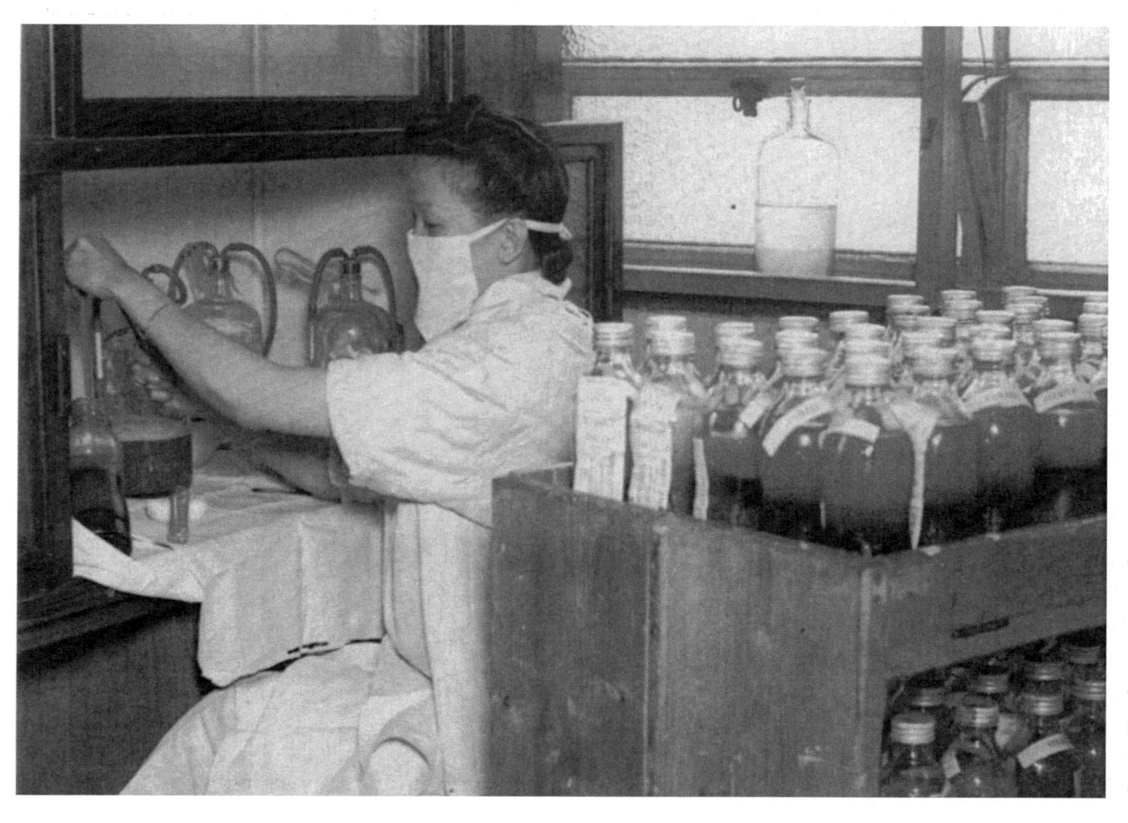

Sheffield Blood Transfusion Centre - by May 1941 Sheffield had 45,000 volunteers enrolled as prospective donors

ARP wardens march past the Town Hall

up and this went on until about 5am. We got all the bins full. The more we swept up, the worst it seemed to get. We'd no gas, no electricity and no water.

"After my mum had hung some curtains over the windows she decided we should better have a rest. She suggested we all laid on the top of a bed upstairs until it got light. But my father said: 'We haven't got time, we start work at eight o'clock'.

"He looked at me and said: 'We might as well sit in the chairs down here' so we did that even though the doors were off. I could feel the draught, it was the middle of December.

"At six o'clock we were leaving for work. My dad said: 'We might have to walk'. We got onto the Woodhead Road that goes down to Bramall Lane.

"No trams of course and nobody about virtually, no shopkeepers about cleaning up and there were loads of windows out. There were just civil defence vehicles and places you could see bombs had dropped.

"When we got to the bottom of London Road there was a tram that had been hit. It had come off the tracks virtually outside where Boston Street is.

"When we got to the bottom of London Road and looked up, the scene was as bad as anything you'd see in Iraq or any other trouble spot you see on TV today. Both sides of The Moor were ablaze and there were fire engines all the way up. There must have been five or six tramcars on fire. So what did we do? We went up The Moor and we're stepping over hoses and we're being told: 'Don't step over this side, go on the other side'. We were criss crossing The Moor and feeling the heat from the fires. The further up we got, the more buildings and tramcars there were on fire.

"I saw fire engines from Chesterfield, Barnsley and other places. They'd fetched them in from all around. There were firemen, police, civil defence workers - dozens and dozens of people.

"We carried on through town and we had to turn left to avoid the site of the bomb that had hit the Marples Hotel. There were a lot of wagons down there. Things carried on right along the Wicker.

"Tramcars were laying almost on the footpath and we were dodging bricks and stones.

"We went up Spital Hill, down Carlisle Street and there was no one about at all. There was no sign of life and it was 24 hour working down there.

"We went to our gate where we'd normally clock in and there was nobody about. We eventually found another gate with a man coming out. He said: 'What are you two doing here?' We said: 'We've come to work in the spring rolling mill'. He said: 'Well you're the first people I've seen today. Not one person has come for the six o'clock shift. When are you two meant to start?' '8 o'clock we said'.

'Well you better go home', he said. 'I can't see work starting again down here for several weeks'.

"We got home and found my mum sat in chair with some blankets over her. This would be about 11 o'clock.

"The corporation came round two or three weeks later putting this tarred paper up at the windows.

"It was light brown on the outside and black on the inside.

"An aunt ended up getting in touch who knew we'd had it bad in that area. She invited us to her house in Malin Bridge. We slept on their floor on the Saturday and Sunday.

"The east end got it on the Sunday, we could see and hear it from where we were. I think it was three or four weeks until we got back to work."

This car was hurled an incredible 65 yards by a bomb blast

What remained of Cockayne's on Snig Hill and Symington & Croft of King Street

Walker & Hall Ltd of Howard Street looked like a collapsed house of cards

CHAPTER FOUR
Sheltering under the burning Central Picture House

All that was left of the Central Picture House on The Moor

Doreen Beeley was on The Moor the night the area was virtually wiped out of existence. Her family was forced to stay in their cinema seats as the raid intensified and ended up sheltering in the downstairs billiards hall.

The Moor was a raging inferno by the time they made their escape. Luckily they survived and were greeted, when they finally got home, by their aunt and uncle. They'd come to Sheffield from London to get a rest from the bombing!

Doreen Beeley said: "That night has remained fresh to me through all these years. My mother took my sister (aged 9) and myself (aged 12) to see Shirley Temple in *The Bluebird* in colour! It was being shown at the Central Picture House which was on The Moor opposite Atkinsons store. It was to be an early Christmas treat as we rarely went out in the evenings. My father was working - he was a wartime policeman, his sight not being good enough for the forces - and was to pick us up when he had finished.

"We settled into our seats but the film had not been going very long when the bumps and bangs from the guns could be heard.

"The manager came onto the screen area and apologised for interrupting but he said it was obvious Sheffield was in for a raid that night and suggested that women and children especially might like to go into the public shelter which was behind the cinema.

"My mother felt we could not go as my father would be unable to find us so we stayed a little longer watching the film.

"The manager went out front again. This time he said it was obviously a serious raid and perhaps those left would like to go downstairs into the billiard hall where he felt it would be safer.

"When we got there we sat on the floor under the tables - I remember the men continued to play - we could hear the balls and see their feet moving round.

"My father finally arrived he said things were bad but at least we were all together now. The manager had more to say. He told us The Moor was ablaze from end to end and it was only a matter of time before the cinema caught fire. He suggested we should make a run for safety.

"I shall never forget the sight that met our eyes as we left the cinema. The Moor was indeed on fire from end to end - there were trams on fire in the middle of the road where they used to run.

"Opposite Atkinsons was terribly damaged and on fire as was Marks and Spencer. Where could we possibly go?

"Dad thought there was a public shelter somewhere near Carver Street so we headed up that way with a small group who came with us, probably because of my father's uniform.

"As we passed Roberts store the windows were not on fire but all the glass had been blown out from all the shops but there a man was helping himself to the fur coats off the models which had been in the window display. Another 'never forget'.

"We were blown off our feet a couple of times as we made our way up the street. You could hear the bombs coming and dad pushed us into a passageway but people were thrown on top of us.

"We all managed to get up and ran forward again. Then a voice: 'Are you looking for shelter?' We were! It was the vicar of the church of St Matthews

"He led us down some steps and under the church into a shelter where we spent the rest of the raid - very frightened - wondering if our house would still be there - listening to the frustrations of the firemen who kept coming in as they had no water to fight the fires as the mains had blown.

"It was chaos but much more quiet than outside with the noise of bombs and fire. A terrifying experience for our family. The 'all clear' went at last and we began our walk home - we were very tired having had no sleep. We lived at Highfields - just off the junction of Abbeydale Road with London Road between the two churches - St. Barnabas and Trinity Methodist. There was broken glass everywhere - our shoes were badly cut - and the horrible smell of burning and soot was everywhere.

"We did not try to go down The Moor, still blazing, but went down the parallel back streets alongside

Shirley Temple's *Blue Bird* which was showing at the Central Picture House on The Moor on the first night of the Sheffield Blitz

"We reached the bottom of Ecclesall Road - huge church damaged there - and turned up London Road and finally our last turn onto Highfield Place.

"We could see from there that there was fire on our road - Belgrave Square - and were thankful to turn the last corner to find our house still there but several of the terrace houses opposite had been burned down. I was very upset as my best friend lived in one of them but we were told everyone had been in their shelters so nobody hurt but everything lost.

"My aunt and uncle were in our house. They had come up from London to get a rest from the bombing! My aunt knew what to do and we benefited from that. She had put out the fire and placed an old sheet in front of the chimney to catch the soot which the bombs had sent tumbling down.

"She was then able to scoop it all up and the room was clean. She had re-lit the fire and got the kettle boiling for a cup of tea which was very welcome.

"She had also filled every bucket and pan with water as there was none on tap by then. We were filthy with the fire and soot but were able to wash before we went wearily to bed. We were without water for several days and had to queue up at the lorries which came each day. No gas for a while either but we had the fire and oven which many houses had in those days. We also had electricity which was amazing and we had an old radiator with one bar which we turned on its back so we could boil a saucepan.

"There was another raid on the Sunday night when they went for their first target and missed - the steel works. We were in our shelters but it was at the other end of the city so much quieter for us. I was surprised at how quickly people set to clearing things up and getting back into a routine. The big stores set up different departments in small shops out of the city centre.

" A night never to forget."

The corner of Fitzalan Square - virtually blitzed out of existence

The damaged Empire Theatre

Looking across a bombsite to Change Alley

CHAPTER FIVE
Doug Lightening - the last of the Blitz firemen

Putting the Blitz fires out was nigh on impossible in many cases

Doug Lightening joined the fire brigade in 1938. Now 94-years-old, he thinks he might be the last surviving fireman that was on duty on both nights of the Sheffield Blitz. He lost a relative in the Marples tragedy and believes no one escaped from the wreckage of the collapsed hotel that received a direct hit at 11.44pm, on Thursday, December 12, 1940.

Doug Lightening said: "Our watch was on days - 7am until 6pm.

"At the time I was staying at my mother in laws home in Wisewood as my wife was expecting our first child (son Richard). He was born on December 10, 1940 - two days before the first night of the Blitz.

"I went home to Far Lane on the Wisewood bus around 6.30pm and started my meal. I remember the sirens going and thought: 'Sod it, I'm going to have my dinner before reporting in'.

"The sirens had been going most nights for weeks as the bombers passed over on their way to Liverpool and Manchester. I walked down to the Auxiliary Fire Service station set up in a garage at the side of the Park Cinema (now a supermarket) and rang through to Division Street, my station and the headquarters for both regular (68 men) and hundreds of full and part time AFS personnel.

"After some bombs dropped in the Hillsborough area, the auxiliary part timers went out.

"Some time later, probably 8pm, I set off and walked into the Division Street station. As I walked I could see the glow of fire from the Ack-ack guns as well as the bombs. The noise of the bombs was deafening. I reported in and after a while I was making a pot of tea when Inspector Outram, 3rd in command, called me over and we went in the second official car, a Hillman 14 HP Saloon, to try and get down to Lady's Bridge in the Wicker. After some detours and some moving of debris to one side we finally got there.

"Two machines were stood there. They had part time AFS crews - one from Lincoln and one from Bolton or Barnsley. They had been trying to lift water from the River Don by suction hose without success. These machines made up for wartime fire fighting were Bedford lorry chassis with a front cab and a large pump (1,000 gallon per minute) mounted at the back of the vehicle.

"Then, with the help of the two crews, we ran lines of hose into Exchange Street and Snig Hill. We fixed a ladder against the skeleton of some flats at the bottom of Snig Hill and I went up with a line of hose and sprayed water onto the roof of the old Police Headquarters which was burning quite fiercely.

"Inspector Outrum said: 'Lightening, I'm leaving you in charge, I'm off.' I sprayed water onto the roof for some three quarters of an hour and then, on seeing the fire was out, came down the ladder. I was knackered.

"After a smoke and a few minutes rest I instructed the AFS men to take a line of hose and tackle the Black Swan pub across the road as it was burning from the top. This was due to incendiary bombs burning downwards and I was worried that the fire would spread along Queen Street. It came to light later that we did stop the fire already up Queen Street but lost the Black Swan pub. I went to the Black Swan bar. It was very hot and the ceiling was starting to burn. With a couple of AFS men we managed to rescue a couple of cases of bottled beer and a carton of Park Drives (200). Shortly after the whole lot fell in.

A member of the fire service tackles a blaze during a October 1941 invasion exercise in Sheffield

"I must explain we only had enough hose for two lines from the river although we had water and capacity for eight lines. We were short of hose. This was the case all over town although other areas were short of water as mains were cut off by bombs. My main concern was to stop the fires spreading from the Black Swan and the buildings at the rear of the old Town Hall and Water Lane police station by concentrating our limited resources for several hours. We did stop these fires from spreading, a very small success amongst a sea of fires and explosions.

"I must confess I was scared most of the time and kept thinking 'this cannot be for real'. There was the constant discomfort and misery of being wet through; the heat scorching you and the pain of cut hands from broken glass everywhere coupled with constant hunger and thirst.

"I did not have a watch at these times so I have little idea what time things happened but sometime, about 5am I think, I was approached by somebody in an AFS steel helmet that was painted bright fire brigade red - everybody else had khaki painted helmets (police had blue).

"The person was extremely agitated and shouted: "Come and see what is happening down the road [Sing Hill]'. I went with him and a row of furniture shops was burning from the top down. I went into the ground floor. It was very hot and the second floor was already well alight. The ground floor was filled with three piece suites, tables and chairs etc.

"I looked into the basement and it was stacked and crammed with suites of bedroom furniture and beds. I told him there was nothing we could do as he was screaming: 'The fire will be into the furniture in no time'. I tried to explain to him that I had one line on the Black Swan which I was not going to move as it was important to hold the first as much as I could there. I added something that made him hopping mad. I suggested he got help and dragged the furniture into the street.

"Subsequently I was summoned to the Watch Room on Saturday morning by Chief Inspector Jack Singleton, second in command. He said: 'I've had a serious complaint about you Lightening" - we were a Police Fire Brigade and had numbers on our collars; we were easy to identify.

"The chap with the furniture problems had

A combined Home Guard/National Fire Service exercise

Regularly referred to as 'The Pig' at the time, this Dennis Rescue Tender was bought by Sheffield Police Fire Brigade in May 1934

reported me and said I'd deliberately let his shops burn down. Jack Singleton said that seeing all Snig Hill was burnt out I could go home and get some sleep - I'd not been home since Thursday evening.

"One of the out of town crew told me that there was dead fireman in a shop doorway. It seemed a piece of shrapnel had hit him under the chin and come out of the top of his steel helmet. It left a hole with the jagged edges facing outwards. I took the helmet which had an AFS number stencilled under the rim and put it on one of the nearby fire machines.

"Later the police came with a lorry to collect dead bodies so I told them where he was and that I'd got his identity number and would report it when I got back to the Central Fire Station.

"In the meantime we were very tired and hungry and I had a brainwave. On the corner of Exchange Street was Davy's General Grocers and Pork Butchers. It was a tall building with the roof off and water pouring down from a water tank in the roof timbers. I was wet through anyway and went in. All the food, bread, confectionery, sausage, bacon etc was ruined with water and debris but under the large counters I found dozens of pork pies - all snug and dry. I got about half a dozen and dashed out of the building. I shared them with eight out of town AFS firemen.

"By this time there was some daylight, it was about 8am and people were starting to come into town, picking their way through the rubble and burnt out cars. Some were 'gob-smacked' when they got to the top of Angel Street and saw the carnage on High Street - burnt out trams and cars; trams and buses shattered.

"When I got back to the station I handed the helmet in with the number on it. The body had been collected by the police and was most likely in the temporary West Street mortuary.

"I was called into the office some days later and asked again about finding the body. It turned out that the helmet was not the one issued to the fireman I found.

"An officer from AFS Headquarters had been round to the house of the man whose number was on the helmet and informed his wife that he had been killed fire fighting in the air raid.

"The horrible twist to the story is that the same day in the evening, the man himself walked into the house to the amazement of his wife and family.

"It seemed that the day before the air raid, two men had been at AFS Headquarters at Bowling Green Street in Sheffield, and had picked up the wrong helmets before leaving.

"So Bowling Green Street had the job of informing the correct family.

"There has always been a lot of speculation about what happened at Marples and a lot of it has been a load of nonsense - I know because I was there and I have a lot of connections with it.

"I was the only regular fireman on Snig Hill with Marples just round the corner. I went up there about nine or ten o clock time and Marples was still there. They'd already dropped a lot of one kilo incendiaries and the place was already on fire.

"The next time I went it had been hit and it was down. Nobody got out of that at all.

"My brother in law's wife used to go in Marples most nights of the week with her mother. They went in there on the night of the Blitz as normal.

"They knew it was burning up above and they'd both had a lot to drink so a lot of them went down into the cellar underneath. The bombs were dropping, it was a about eleven o'clock and her mother suddenly said: 'I'm off'. The daughter wouldn't come but her mother walked home in the Blitz. Of course the daughter didn't turn up and next day the mother went into town to see what was left of the Marples.

"She rang my brother in law who was in the RAF, he got home leave and came back to Sheffield to see me. I went with him to the temporary mortuary up West Street way where a lot of the bodies were. They'd excavated the place and this would have been a week after the Blitz. They showed us the bodies from the Marples and you'd never have known they were people. They were just little lumps burnt away. Bloke in charge said: 'There was nobody that came out.' What they did have was a box of rings and bangles that women had worn.

"As far as I can say, when it was hit with the bomb, there was nobody in there that could have survived as they'd dropped bombs on the fires.

"Pictures appeared of people walking out but that was actually a picture of an air raid shelter and somebody had assumed they were coming out of Marples.

"I went up again about 5 or 6am and there were burnt out trams, buses and overhead wires all mangled up from the trams. It was just a total mess and at that time when I went up there was a big stores on there called Walsh's. The store was still up when I went up earlier on but when I went up again it was burning well down. To be truthful, on

Capt. Clement Roberts MBE and officers of the ARP

that night, there were very few fires put out.

"It was a long and terrible night, the 12/13th December 1940.

"The following Sunday we went on duty as usual but everybody was expecting another air raid as Lord Haw Haw told us so and everyone listened to the German broadcasts of the time.

"We were told on Sunday afternoon that the day shifts were not going off duty at 6pm but would also be on the night shift as another German air raid was expected."

Men and equipment poured into the blazing city

The ranks of the fire service increased to an estimated 1,800 in the Sheffield Blitz.

At 12:42am on the 13th December Sheffield Police Fire Brigade requested assistance from neighbouring fire brigades.

Their call was heeded from as far away as Manchester and Nottingham as men and equipment poured into the blazing city.

Manned pumps arrived from Mexborough, Wortley, Hoyland, Kiveton Park, Thorne, Wath, Cudworth, Pudsey, Morley, Spenborough, Pontefract, Shipley, Bingley, Keighley, Brighouse, Elland, Holmfirth, Castleford, Mirfield and Ossett.

Manchester and Nottingham sent ten pumps each, Bradford sent six, Barnsley four, Doncaster, Wakefield, Halifax, and Huddersfield sent three each, and Rotherham, Wombwell, Leeds and York all sent two.

The outside help totalled 70 pumps and 522 men.

It's hard to imagine the carnage endured by the fire crews. Many of the pumps, understandably, had difficulty getting into the city at all and had to be guided round gaping bomb craters and blazing buildings.

Services were hampered further by the cold December weather that caused water, where it was available, to freeze.

Many of these men were simply people in reserved occupations who thought it their duty to help.

Third officer Christopher Eyre and his colleague's accounts haven't been published for nearly seventy years.

He said:

"If a man who went through it all tells you he wasn't afraid that night you can take it he's lying. At first it wasn't so bad, though bad enough. We were turned out right at the start to save the Empire, and fought the fire there for an hour.

"Then the bombs started falling all along The Moor. It's almost impossible to describe. We could hear the whistling and the crashes, we were ringed in by flame, and yet I seemed to be in a vacuum.

"You had to concentrate with all you'd got on the job and ignore what was happening within yards of you.

"Even the "regulars" had never fought these conditions before. But there were only 60 of them and the 1,800 strong fire fighting force was mainly made up of shopkeepers, businessmen and workers in "reserved occupations" whose experience had been confined to backyard bonfires before the war.

"I remember looking down The Moor once and seeing the whole place alight from end to end with buildings collapsing into the street. Now and again we dived under the appliance as a big one whistled down beside us, and once I was blown on my back without receiving a scratch. The team was directing its hoses on to the furiously blazing Campbell's furniture store. Without let-up the waves of bombers were pouring down their loads.

"From one end to the other the firemen on The Moor were straddled by bomb-bursts.

"While we were fighting the fires in Pinstone Street one of our chaps came to tell me that one appliance which had gone to Porter Street had been blown to bits. Two men went with it, both my close friends.

"Later in the night we were fighting a tremendous fire at Bramall Lane, but lack of water sometimes made it impossible to do anything.

"We were using anything on wheels to draw the pumps, driving over the debris where it was possible and with hardly any idea of what streets were blocked or open."

AFS Fireman Bill Wright said:

"Woodhouse fire station received the call to send four machines to Sheffield, leaving one to cover Woodhouse.

"I was driver and pump operator on the first machine. On reaching the top of Normanton Hill, Jerry saw our headlights and started diving and firing tracer bullets at our machines. We managed to get through to the bottom of Granville Road, where we met an amazing sight. Tramcars and overhead wires were all over the road. We carried on to Fitzalan Square, where the Marples public house had just received a direct hit. We placed three machines on The Moor and one down Porter Street.

"On The Moor, tramcars were blazing away,

Capt. J. Kenny and Officers - Civil Defence - Ambulance Service

shops were ablaze and an old ex-fireman, a Woodhouse man, Ike Fielding, fetched me down The Moor to one fire. There were wax models of women, with very expensive gowns on, melting away in the window, and old Ike was telling me his wife could not afford a frock.

"The Blitz started on Thursday night and we were down there until Sunday dinner time when we got the order from HQ that all fires were out and to return to home stations.

"The best sight I remember was going back up City Road with people lining the pavements and cheering us all the way to Intake."

Ambulance driver W. H. Livsey was having tea at the George Hotel in Hathersage after a run out to Bakewell just two hours before the bombs started falling on Thursday, December 12.

Here's his story:

5:00 pm

"Afternoon - V. Brammer & girlfriend, Phyl and I went for run to Bakewell. We had tea at the George Hotel, Hathersage. The waitress speaking of the recent bombings said that the Germans would not find Sheffield. It was the best blackout city in England. So an airman friend of hers had told her."

6:30 pm

"There was a slight mist when I arrived home at Uplands, which is at the side of Sugworth Hall, off Sugworth Road, Bradfield, Sheffield. I went in for a warm before getting the new car out and going into work for the 10pm to 7am shift."

7:05 pm

"I started the car up, and Joan on hearing this said it was sounded like an aeroplane. I laughed but then heard an explosion in Sheffield, so I decided to wait at home for a bit. From the field at the back I could see huge fires which I thought were over the east end works. Brilliant flares were dropping and floating slowly to earth. Our anti-aircraft batteries were trying to shoot these out. Tracer bullets could be seen, and the enemy were evidently trying to shoot down the barrage balloons. The noise was terrific. The gun nearest our house changed its firing direction and fired out over our house to meet the incoming planes. There wasn't a minute that passed without the crash of bombs over Sheffield.

"About midnight there was a slight lull in the bombing, so I suggested setting off with the car, but the attack started again. I waited whilst 1:25 am and then decided that the huge fires to be seen were not over Crosspool, so we should travel that far and investigate.

"Passing Moscar Top saw two cars smashed up.

"When I had just passed Blackbrook, shells were bursting above us so I pulled up and sat under a wall until guns changed their trajectory. Seeing as it was quiet for a moment I made a dash for Crosspool leaving V. Brammer at Coldwell Lane.

"Watching for shell bursts near the Sportsman Inn, I failed to notice debris in the road, the result of a landmine in Cardoness Road and I nearly turned the car over.

"I arrived at Watt Lane. Phyl's mother and father were next door at the Bradshaw's. I told them of the damage in Manchester Road and Benty Lane. I borrowed Phyl's tin hat and set off for town. The police stopped me at the Kings Head, as I was running without lights. I saw a huge explosion down at Broomhill, and I got the wind up and went to Lydgate Lane Ambulance Station. All their ambulances were out of service through crashes and burst tyres due to glass.

"There was no chance of a lift to town, so I decided to try again. I got as far as Oak Park when I saw soldiers rushing out of Tapton House Road.

"I pulled into the side of the road, opened the car door, and was about to get out when a bomb, exploding at the back of Redlands, lifted my car on to its side and threw me out on to the causeway. I was only shaken and five soldiers helped me put the car back on four wheels again, and luckily it still ran. The front wheels were a little damaged and petrol had spilled out of the tank but it was still serviceable.

"Next I went as far as the York Hotel at Broomhill.

"The house next door but one to Col. Lycett's, was on fire. I next turned down Glossop Road, and saw St Mark's Church was on fire.

"A bomb had dropped on my right down Newbould Lane, and about at Wilkinson Street I saw a huge fire in front of me (Reuben Thompson's Garage), so I turned left and went up to the University and turned to go down Brook Hill. A crater the width of the road stopped me, so I backed up and went down Leavygreave Road where I had to bump over fire hoses. There was a small fire at Jessop's Hospital, and I turned down Gell Street into West Street and travelled as far as Regent Street, where the Boots chemist shop had received a hit. Toilet rolls were all over the place having been blown out of the window. I turned up Regent Street (as West Street was littered with broken glass,) and across Broad Lane into Red Lane. On passing St. Vincent's church a stained glass window was blown out in front of me. I came out near the bus sheds, and they were backlit with fire. Church Street, Campo Lane and St. James Row were a mass of flames. I got as far as Scotland Street and became entangled in tram wires, the car engine stopped, and as I got out to restart it the new police station received a direct hit and instantly became a mass of flames. I just got the car into reverse to back round to Scotland Street when Shaw's newsagents blew up twenty yards in front of me.

"The blast blew me back to Solly Street. I got up Scotland Street and turned down Lambert Street when three explosions blew out the windows of the flats, some debris dropped on the back of the car but did not stop me.

"I came out into Gibraltar Street, and I was stopped by a convoy of fire tenders from Huddersfield and Dewsbury. They were stopped by a huge pile of three tramcars piled in a heap. A bomb had dropped on top of them. The officer-in-charge wanted to know how to get to the Central Fire Station. I directed them and noticed a big black Rolls Royce car and trailer, which I afterwards saw in St. Mary's Road all smashed up.

"Crossing the road I went across Spring Street and arrived at the Central Ambulance Station. I parked "Thunderbolt" under the shed and went into the shelter under Mellows where the staff were. As I went down the steps a fire bomb landed on the roof of Mellows and started a big fire. After reporting to Capt. Kenny I went upstairs again and found the whole of the building above a mass of flames.

"The heat was unbearable. I turned on the hosepipe and sprayed the petrol pump and my own car and pushed it as far from the flames as possible. The fire brigade arrived but could not get water so went away. I was sent to Oxford Street Chapel with two ARP Girls as attendants on ambulance 340.

"I arrived to find it had received a direct hit and that a number or people were buried in the houses below. An old man, who said his family were under the first house, told me they had pleaded with him to stay with them in the cellar, but he would not and so lived to tell the tale. As there was no chance of getting at them for some time I went back to Corporation Street.

"In Spring Street I met Capt. Kenny who sent me to Shoreham Street tram sheds for a number of cases. I got three of them alive, one of the fire attendants told me she lived next to the Cathedral in the Church House and that all her people were there, so I decided to run round and see what had happened at Church Street and St. James Row.

"They were burning fiercely. The nearest we could get was Leopold Street so the ambulance was parked and I asked a fireman if it was safe to go. He said no, but after explaining, he said he would help us but that we went at our own risk. This made me laugh. It seemed strange somehow in the middle of an air raid.

"We found the house shattered but only one old man was injured so he was taken with the rest to the Royal Hospital. These two jobs, although not far from the station, took three times as long to reach as it was impossible to travel along nine out of every ten roads. After unloading my patients I saw

Harry Beck (another driver) behind the hospital door sobbing. Thinking it was an attack of nerves I took no notice of him, but on entering the Lodge I learned he had just been told his brother George (another driver) and Percy Wood his attendant had been killed. Attendant Dolphin who had been with Harry came with me and as we set off for Carwood Avenue the 'All Clear' went. The raid had been in progress for ten hours.

"On arrival we found that the casualties were all people in the air raid shelters. Out of about fifteen Anderson Shelters, all built without blast walls and containing three or four people each, only two were alive. These we taken to Fulwood Annex, the Royal being full.

"On returning to the station we were sent to Reginald Street where the rescue parties had recovered some bodies - two alive and one dead.

"They were taken to the Royal Hospital. Taking the bodies to the mortuary we found that out of fifty three bodies only seven had been identified. The bodies of some AFS firemen were in canvas bags, not much bigger than sand bags, they could not be recognised as men.

"As it was now about 12:15 pm, I packed up and went home."

AFS Fireman Jack Gee said of his experiences:

"On Thursday, 12th December, 1940, I was on duty at Archer Road Fire Station and we were turned out to the city centre. At that time I was living in the neighbourhood around St. Mary's Church at the bottom of The Moor. As we drove down London Road, I could see that all that area had been flattened by bombs. I couldn't help worrying about my wife and wondering whether she was safe. But there was nothing I could do about it.

"We were fighting fires at Moorhead when our machine took a direct hit. Those of the crew who were not killed outright were badly injured. As I lay on the pavement trying to recover my senses, I realised that my left arm was in a terrible state.

"Eventually someone pulled me away to the shelter of the doorway of the Empire Theatre. Then I was taken down to an air raid shelter. I was there about three hours and the people in the shelter covered me up. I was suffering from shock and cold. A woman actually sent her fur coat down to cover me up but I sent it back. After two or three hours, some people enquired if any injured firemen were there. It was the ambulance men and they put me on a stretcher in a loading bay. In actual fact we came through the loading bay of Burtons the Tailors to get onto the road itself, which was Porter Street. Then one man came back and told us to hang on a minute as the Germans were machine gunning.

"We stayed in the loading bay for a few minutes and we could hear machine gun bullets hitting the brickwork. By this time we could not hear any of our anti-aircraft guns firing from the gun sites around the city. They had probably run out of ammunition.

"They were all silent after about two o'clock and the planes were coming over unmolested.

"They initially got me into an ambulance which was parked on The Moor. There was a girl in the ambulance of about eighteen years-old.

"She was with the ambulance crew and sat in the ambulance all the time. We went down The Moor and practically the whole of The Moor was ablaze. We twisted and turned and I found out that the driver had to detour and go up so many streets to try and get down The Moor. Eventually we went up Ecclesall Road to get to the Royal Hospital (situated on Devonshire Street and now demolished). The girl sat there all the time. She was as cool as anything and never budged.

"When we arrived at the Royal Hospital, we entered at the back entrance in Eldon Street.

"All the windows were out and the nurses were moving about with hand torches. They were trying to find out where everybody was. They told the ambulance men to take me on to Jessops Hospital but the ambulance men told them that there was no chance of getting up there. While they were arguing, I heard a voice saying: 'I know who you are, but where are you from?' I realised that they were talking to Bill Jones, another crew member, who had been picked up at the top of The Moor and had arrived just before me. So I put them right as to where he was from.

"At about 4 o'clock in the morning, they were able to put the lights on in the hospital. I looked around me and saw that there were rows and rows of beds and stretchers toe to toe, all jam packed together.

"They were taking the most serious cases first.

"These were put on a table and given a general anaesthetic, using ether. After my operation I came to in a bed with my left arm stuck out like a birdcage.

"The next day Bill and I expected people to come from the station, but no one came. We finished up in a ward with four other firemen but we were unable to find anything out from anyone. Eventually, some scouts came round the ward to ask if any patients wanted errands done. They said they would do them. By this time, two days had gone by since the night of the bombing and remembering the damage in the St. Marys Road area where I lived, I was worried about my wife. So I got one of the scouts to go down there and see if he could find out anything about what had happened. When he came back, it was not good news. He said that my house had been bombed and there was nobody there. The whole area was more or less devastated. That was a very worrying time for me.

"On Saturday night around 9 o'clock, the nurse came in and said: 'Mr. Gee, we've got a surprise for you. Here is your wife!'

"My wife had been trying to find me, and I had been trying to find her. The whole of our house had been destroyed, and there was hardly anything left.

"Since then, my wife had been running round the fire stations trying to find out what had happened to me.

"We got another air raid on the Sunday night. We were still in the Royal Hospital and we thought the bombs were landing close by. It did sound like it.

"We had a gunner in with us from the Norton Gun Site with damage to his ears. He told us that they were not bombs but guns and not very far away.

"We laughed at him over this but we found out from the vicar of Fulwood that there was a gun sited outside the hospital. It turned out a convoy of forty guns had been shipped into Sheffield that very day, so they must have known that another raid was coming. Guns were put on street intersections

"There was another one outside the Somme Barracks on Glossop Road.

"The Sheffield raid on the Thursday night was the longest single raid of the war. Coventry and one or two other places were more concentrated but did not last as long. The Sheffield raid last from 7 o'clock in the evening until 4 o'clock the next morning, and for the last four hours we had no defences. There was a story that a lorry and trailer were seen fully loaded with shells on East Bank Road, looking for the Norton Gun Site. I don't know if they ever got there. The raid on Sunday, 15th December, wasn't as long. I think the Germans got a shock when all those guns opened up. It must have deterred them somewhat.

"A week later, the cases that the doctors thought were going to be a long while recovering, were moved from the city hospitals. Obviously, the authorities were expecting more raids. I was taken to Wakefield to a hospital which had previously been a mental hospital. At the beginning of the war, the mental patients had been transferred to other institutions and then this one had been opened up as a military hospital.

"At this time there were more civilians injured than military so they began to admit civilians as well. I was up there three or four months. After Bill Jones had been in hospital two days he got gangrene and they had to take his leg off. Doctor Forbes, the Police Surgeon, examined us and he decided whether or not we would be fit to return to service. After eight weeks, Bill Jones was given his discharge. If there was any doubt, it was possible to have a thirteen week period before the doctor made a final decision. I got a letter sent to my house after thirteen weeks giving me my discharge."

"Fire Fighting Heroes of the Blitz"

An article by Star newspaper reporter T.H. Cramb published on the 9th October, 1944, included a vivid description of the events of the nights of the 12th and 13th December 1940.

He said: "There are several details of the Sheffield Blitz, December 1940, which have never come to light. Some never will, but one service which had many heroes during the rain of fire and destruction on the city was the fire service.

"Some of the work which the Auxiliary Fire Service - as it was then known - performed that night can now be told.

"Heroism, devotion to duty, service under difficulties, undaunted spirits, and hard work all rolled into one aptly describes those firemen's night way back in 1940.

"They were called and not found wanting. They answered the call of the sirens, they stood their ground, and they did their best. Appliances got stuck in bomb craters. In some cases the crews managed to get them out; others had to be left as they were damaged.

"One pump received a direct hit as it was working and three of the crew were killed and another injured, while another pump was wrecked by the blast of a nearby bomb.

"During the night five members of the Service were killed and 56 injured, 12 of them seriously - a very small number considering the total number of personnel actively engaged during the raid.

"Information had been received earlier in the evening that Sheffield was likely to receive a strong visit from the Luftwaffe that night, with the result that as much preparedness as possible was made."

Call for help

"Within a very short time all were engaged on fires raised by the enemy in all parts of the city, and a district call was sent out for additional help.

"That help first came from Rotherham, Barnsley, Doncaster, Mexborough, Wortley, Kiveton Park, Cudworth, Thorne, Wath, Hoyland and Wombwell, but as the raid developed a regional call brought assistance from Chesterfield, Leeds, Bradford, Wakefield, Manchester, Nottingham, Lincoln, Sleaford, Birmingham and Grantham.

"Owing to the system then in force, all the outside brigades had to report to the Headquarters in Division Street, Sheffield, and it speaks well for the authorities when it is said that all reported safely, and were immediately dispatched to fire zones without loss, or incident.

"The first calls were to Hounsfield Road and to the Neepsend district.

"Within a short space, however, no fewer than 550 calls were received by telephone at the control room in Division Street.

"As fast as reinforcements arrived there was a task waiting for them. Much of the smartness of the outside brigades in arriving at their allotted fire zones was due to about 20 members of the Sheffield Transport Department.

"Tram drivers, bus drivers, and conductors unable to do anything with their own vehicles, offered themselves as guides to outside brigades and directed them to the incidents. Those few can be classed among the unsung heroes of the night.

"Thousands of fires were breaking out in various parts of the city, and many an engine and pump crew dealt with several outbreaks other than the one they were sent to.

"Half an hour after sounding the alert the AFS met their first big set-back. Water ceased to be obtainable from the mains, and quick thinking had to be done to keep most of the machines supplied."

Water from Don

"Public baths and the few emergency tanks in existence were tapped and the water relayed. Water was also relayed some distance from the River Don. Many fires were kept in check by water which had accumulated in bomb craters adjoining burst mains, and many lines were kept operating by the fire float on the canal. It is estimated that

ARP protective headgear for steelworkers

well over 36 miles of hose were in use that night, in addition to several miles attached and operated by industrial fire brigades.

"Those industrial brigades pulled their weight, and gave useful assistance in all sorts of ways to the AFS. One remarkable feature of the whole night was the fact that the telephone system of the fire brigade continued working throughout the whole raid, this despite the fact that two stations received hits, these being Sharrow Vale and Hoyle Street."

Brave Canadian

"What few civilians there were about in the streets in the thick of the raid gave useful assistance to the pump crews in helping to run out hose and in many other ways. Tribute must be paid to the Canadian soldier who perched himself on the dome of the Empire Theatre and played a hose on the raging fire at Campbell's furniture store - which, incidentally, was the first real big fire of the raid.

"Hundreds of fires were reported by people who had seen reflections of other fires in house and shop windows, and calls were also received for fire engines to stand by at business premises 'just in case.'"

Nurse fought fire

"Nether Edge Hospital received a bad hit, and fire was raging in one quarter - yet the firemen found a small nurse tackling it on her own with a bucket of water and a stirrup pump.

"Two small boys, acting as volunteer messengers in one part of the city, put out numerous incendiaries, and then curled themselves up by a pump and went fast asleep - tired out and oblivious of bombs dropping in the vicinity.

"One woman, with sandbags under her arms, followed the firemen into one building and dropped her sand on every little outbreak she passed and then went outside for more sandbags. She would not listen to orders to get to safety.

"The following morning another problem faced the authorities - food for the crews. Certain arrangements had been made but these were planned around the city receiving the all clear.

"Anyway, one station was immediately turned into an eating house, volunteers arrived and in a very quick time all had a hot breakfast.

"In addition, several large houses - businesses and private - devoted all their time to supplying food to the AFS, while the YWCA in Division Street immediately opened the premises as sleeping quarters, crews falling asleep in their soaked and mud spattered clothes.

"What few women had then joined the AFS stuck to their tasks throughout the night, and refused to be relieved when the raid was really heavy."

Civilians helped

"A feature of the two raids, as seen by AFS officers and men, was that whereas on the first night civilians were under cover as much as possible, they were out and about on the Sunday night, ready to give the brigade any assistance they could.

"As one officer put the position the first night: 'When the all clear sounded the earth seemed to belch forth thousands of people, just like ants coming from underground.

"'They were silent and the only noise was the roaring of the flames and the crunching of the broken glass under the people's feet.

"'It was uncanny; those silent thousands emerged from apparently nowhere."

"'The Sunday was the opposite. Those same people came out and offered to brave all the dangers in their anxiety to lend a hand.'"

Lord Mayor of Sheffield, Alderman J. A. Longden speaking to members of the Home Guard in Norfolk Park

CHAPTER SIX
Chandeliers shake at Sheffield City Hall

Marching past the City Hall

Frank Gummer was under manager of Sheffield City Hall in December 1940, he'd worked his way through the ranks since the day the building was first unveiled in 1932.

He remembered Thursday, December 12, 1940 was the night that time nearly ran out for the iconic building.

Frank Gummer was doing his utmost to calm the 250 customers in the building as all hell was breaking loose outside.

He remembered: "The chandeliers were swinging and the front entrance had been blown in. The customers sheltered in the ballroom and had a sing-song and played lotto and dominoes to keep their spirits up."

Though an emergency water tank shielded the bomb blast that would have otherwise wiped the building off the face of the earth, Sheffield City Hall didn't escape the tragedy of war.

War weapons week exhibition ends in death

Probably the biggest war tragedy relating to the building cannot be blamed solely on Hitler.

Though the accident would never have happened if it hadn't been for war, the circumstances around the deaths of a 14-year-old boy scout and an

18-year-old youth haunted the building for years after.

They were killed by an anti-tank rifle that was fired accidently in the War Weapons Exhibition. Three other people were injured in the process.

A newspaper report said: "The gun was one of a number of weapons, ancient and modern, exhibited with a view to arousing public interest in the city's successful attempt to raise £4,000,000. How the accident happened is a mystery."

The dead were Gordon Strange (14), 99 Hartley Brook Road, Sheffield and Alan Raymond Tucker (18), 129 Sheffield Road, Woodhouse.

"The noise of the explosion was terrific", said one man present.

"When the reverberations died down there were screams of agony. Women were crying and trembling."

Change Alley and the King's Head Hotel

Nellie's war memories start at Armistice Day in 1918

Broomgrove Nursing Home's oldest and longest standing resident has vivid recollections of the attacks in December 1940.

97-year-old Nellie Bennett's war memories actually begin a lot further back. She can still recall Armistice Day in 1918 as a little girl.

But it is the horrors of the Sheffield Blitz and its aftermath that are as poignant today as they ever were.

She said: "I can still remember children coming into the shelter screaming. We lived opposite Ellesmere Road School in Pitsmoor and spent Blitz night in the boiler house of the school. The noise of the bombs got gradually worse and the ground would shake - I can still remember the 'whooshing' sound they made.

"I slept on a door that night and had to go to walk to work the next day. The devastation was terrible.

"I can remember the next morning walking through High Street. It was absolutely awful.

"There were trams on their side, their lines were all twisted, Walsh's was a blaze and the police kept re-directing you. I ended up walking from Pitsmoor to Broomhill that morning.

"On the Sunday night we got it again. It was really, really bad. But when you're young you somehow take these things in your stride.

Married in 1939, the year the war broke out, Nellie had her wedding reception at Stephenson's Restaurant on Castle Street in the city centre in the midst of the blackout. "It was all a bit strange but we still enjoyed it", she said.

Her fellow Broomgrove resident Joy Newton, 85-years-old, described the scenes she saw in the immediate aftermath of the bombing as 'like watching a horror film - it looked like the end of the world. It almost didn't seem real'.

A massive explosion near to her Broomhill home in 1940 has stayed with her to this day.

She said: "I was terrified. I've had a lifelong fear of explosions and bangs. I hid on my bunk under a red blanket.

"When the sirens went it was initially very quiet. My father let me look out of an open window with him and the planes sounded as though they were a long way away. Suddenly I was blown to the floor.

"I think it was the blast from a parachute mine that landed on Westbourne Road nearby."

A life of torment followed Blitz family deaths

Douglas Oldfield initially thought he'd done well to survive the attacks but the death of his sister's family and her lifetime of torment have stayed with him forever: "I lived near Empire Road, just off Abbeydale Road and we had a time bomb that dropped in our backyard. It's a good job it was a time bomb or else me and my brother wouldn't have survived. In those days you either had an Anderson Shelter or a strengthened cellar and we had a strengthened cellar.

"It was a miracle we survived. They had to evacuate the whole area.

"My sister and her family lived in the Division Street area. Their house had a direct hit. My sister survived. She was buried under the debris.

"They had to dig her out. They only found parts of her husband. It was the same with their son and daughter. The daughter was about a year and ten months old and the son about five years-old.

"My sister never got over it. Her nerves were totally shattered. She had to go in Middlewood mental home."

Betty Ralph, now 84, was one of the hundreds who took their chances and stayed in their cinema seats after the sirens went off. At only thirteen years of age and on her own, you can only imagine her fear as the bombs started dropping and the Air Raid Warden refused to let her out.

Betty Ralph said: "I always went to the Abbeydale Picture House twice a week. I always went on a Thursday on my own after I'd had my tea and I was in there when the sirens went. Not many people took any notice, seven o'clock it was. By five past I could hear bombs dropping. They wouldn't let us out, the wardens made us all go downstairs into the ballroom. I was there until half past seven the following morning. You can imagine how my mother was feeling.

"She lived just a bit further down from the Abbeydale Picture House on the right hand side.

"At the side of our house was a fairly large bake house called Arnold Myers. That had had a direct hit. My mother was in the cellar at the time with my dad - it had been reinforced. It had been made into a public air raid shelter - three cellars knocked into one. She must have been demented with worry about me.

"After a few hours I tried to get out but the air raid warden said: 'No you are not leaving.' And I said: 'Well I only live a few yards down there'. And he said: 'No because the incendiary bombs are dropping all over the place.

"When I got out I saw a burned out tram on Abbeydale Road.

"We ended up having to move to Totley to live with my auntie. She was only in a corporation house and she wasn't very pleased about it.

"I can remember the biggest hole I have ever seen between Gatefield Road and Marden Road.

"It would have held two buses. So that area was all blocked off.

"We were out of it in Totley for the second night of the Sheffield Blitz that hit the east end.

"I ended up leaving school at 14 years-old and working at Walsh's. They'd opened several little

The King and Queen touring bombed out Sheffield

branches after their original premises had been destroyed in the Blitz. They had one on Fargate opposite Davy's Victoria Cafe and I worked there. I worked on the stockings department.

"I was on that counter when the very first nylons came in. We only got so many. I think they came from America. We used to get a lot of very well to do ladies coming in for them. I've still got a pair upstairs at home!"

Gerald Cartwright, now 83, was in the Sheffield Empire on the first night of the Sheffield Blitz.

He said: "We were in the Empire watching Henry Hall on the night of the Sheffield Blitz. I was eleven at the time.

"We heard the bombs dropping and were ushered downstairs.

"Some people left for the Porter Street public shelter. I'm glad we stayed because many of them were killed.

"Everyone left their seats in a very orderly fashion. I think the decision was taken to end the show when the conditions got too serious.

"There were a couple of jugglers on that night - I understand one was killed.

"Henry Hall and his band were with us. I remember leaving the Empire around 4am after the all clear.

"The nearby furniture store was destroyed. The Moor was utter devastation. My brother worked at Atkinsons at the time - I remember saying to him: 'You won't be going to work tomorrow'. Their store was completely destroyed.

"We walked home to Ecclesall. We had to tread carefully down The Moor. Buildings burned to either side of us. Trams were wrecked."

Gerald's parents didn't stay around for the second night of the Sheffield Blitz.

"My mother packed us in the car and we went to Fox House for the night!", he said.

Les Dinsdale said: "I'd gone for a drink in town with my friend. We didn't shelter, we ended up walking about six miles home. We walked up all the back roads that we knew. I was a bit nervous. One night I was in the Coliseum and it started again. You could hear the shells on the roof.

"Sheffield was left in a mess. Tramlines were torn up and everything. "

The City Hall Ballroom was turned into a feeding station for Sheffield's bombed out citizens

CHAPTER SEVEN
Carnage at the Marples

High Street is devastated

No name is more synonymous with the Sheffield Blitz than the Marples Hotel. The seven storey Fitzalan Square hostelry was the scene of the biggest single tragedy of the attacks.

An estimated 70 people died. Bodies still remain buried there to this day.

Marie Parkin's dad was only a few yards away from the Marples Hotel when it was hit. Luckily, he lived to tell the tale.

She said: "My father was in town all night working at the telephone switchboard at the GPO in Fitzalan Square.

"He tried to come home to us (at Ecclesall) but as he got up those steps by the Post Office the bomb dropped on Marples and the blast blew him back down to the bottom.

"He then had to wait to the 'all clear' before setting off home again.

"When he eventually managed to get home (about 9.30am) - whacked of course - he came in and said: 'Atkinsons has gone, C&A's has gone, Central Picture Palace has gone and loads more'.

"He told us he was walking past the college on Ecclesall Road (by Collegiate Crescent) and an air raid warden shouted: 'Watch out, there are two dead bodies there'.

"He explained that a plane had swooped down and emptied its machine gun along there. You can still see the holes in the college wall!

"A very stark reminder of the Blitz."

'Arms and legs blown off - dead bodies everywhere'

Emmie Gommersall came out of Heeley Palace cinema to witness the Luftwaffe planes roaring overhead and incendiary bombs dropping as far as the eye could see. She saw the aftermath of the carnage at the Marples Hotel and witnessed the shocking horror of broken bodies strewn around the city centre.

Emmie Gommersall [nee Pike] said:

"December 1940 was the month we all realised what war was. It was a Thursday evening and I had gone to the pictures with Alice, one of my boyfriend Herbert's sisters. We had only been in ten minutes when the film went off and we were told to evacuate the building.

"Alice and I came out of the Heeley Palace that was on Heeley Bottom and ran up Gleadless Road, planes roaring above and incendiary bombs dropping everywhere. About 100 yards further on we ran up a passage and into the first house we came to which had had its door blown off and had no windows. We heard people in the cellar and asked if we could join them and they said: 'Yes, yes'.

"So we had to stay there all night until the all clear went the next morning. We came out to fires burning everywhere where houses had been bombed. I went home with Alice and then walked back to my mums. Everywhere was burning. We lived in Thorpe Road, five minutes from Bramall Lane football ground which was ablaze. As we got nearer home I was dreading what I would find.

"Thank god my family were all safe. My dad had gone to see if he could help anyone. He came home with a couple and their four children who had lost everything - their home and all their possessions. It was heartbreaking to see them.

"The man was a postman just like my dad. They stayed in our front room for three months until they were rehoused. That's what people did in those days.

"We had no water to wash until stand pipes were brought round, no electricity or gas.

"I set off to work. I managed a fruit and vet shop at Hillsborough Corner. What a trek to walk from Highfields to work. There were no trams as the tram lines were all down. As I walked through the city centre I could not believe what I saw. Arms and legs blown off, dead bodies everywhere. It made me feel sick. Volunteers trying to help anyone that might still be alive.

"When I reached the Marples on the corner of Fitzalan Square it was just rubble, bodies all over it. It had had a direct hit. The crater was that large it was impossible to remove all the bodies - there was still some buried to this day.

Looking across the Marples bombsite towards the devastated markets area

"When I finally arrived at work all the shop windows were blown out. There was debris everywhere. They came round and boarded up the shop windows and people wrote on them: 'Bombed But Not Beaten'. That was the British spirit.

"On Sunday night Jerry was back, down the east end that time. Attercliffe was their target as the large steel works were all in that area. It was to be the second night of destruction.

"We had no phones in our homes. Then only posh people had them, but Herbert always rang me on Sunday afternoon from the phone box at the top of our road at 3pm. I waited until 5.30pm on the Sunday. When he finally got through, worried sick he was, he had heard on the radio in Scotland about the bombings in Sheffield; he was only on a few minutes when the sirens started, so back home I went and into the shelter until 6am next morning. Life went on, day after day, going to work and queuing for hours for food.

"1941 came and on Easter Monday that year Herbert and I got married at St. Barnabas Church in Highfields. No white dress for me (not enough coupons). I bought a nice suit I could wear after. My mum put a spread on for us best she could. No wedding cake, instead a homemade sponge cake.

"Later that evening we went to the Railway Pub on the corner of Bramall Lane with our families (it had been repaired after the previous bombings).

"Herbert had just got up to sing 'Two little girls in blue' (he had a wonderful singing voice), and then the bloody sirens went off. We all had to run into the public dug out round the corner. Incendiary bombs dropping everywhere, we never got to hear Herbert sing properly. I can smile about it you know, what a way to spend a wedding night!"

A chance change in shifts ensured Barry Baxter's dad survived the Marples tragedy and was working when the seven storey venue collapsed like a house of cards.

He said: "During the war my late father worked at Fox's Steel Works in Stocksbridge. One day he asked a mate to swap shifts from mornings to afternoons.

"The same night Marples Hotel was bombed. This was my father's friend's local. They would have been dancing there that night if he hadn't changed his shift. Whenever they met in town he would buy my father a drink."

George Turner spent the first night of the attacks in the family's air raid shelter on Madehurst Road, Heeley. He said:

"On the night of 12th December 1940, I was nearly 6-years-old. That night the sirens sounded and my mother, sister, brother and I went to our air raid shelter in our back garden at 48 Madehurst Road.

"As the night went on we could hear the sound of bombs being dropped and exploding and, on one occasion, we heard a terrific blast as one bomb dropped less than 200 yards away outside number 361 Myrtle Road (the home of an old man living alone named Mr Miller). The bomb left a massive crater in Myrtle Road, the road above where we lived. The all clear siren went and we all went back indoors. As I was walking along the path outside our house - we had a small brick wall stretching around one side of the house - I heard a loud pinging noise.

George Turner's family: (left to right) his father (George Henry Turner), sister (Lilian Rita), brother (Derek William Burton Turner), George Turner and mother (Eva Caroline Turner).

"We went into our house and could see the town centre was ablaze from an upstairs window, namely Walsh's (where T J Hughes now stands), Marples public house and several other shops in that vicinity. The following morning I examined the drain pipe from where the pinging noise had originated, and I found a piece of shrapnel below the drain pipe in question. The pipe had a hole in it. The following morning I heard that a bomb had dropped in Myrtle Road and my mother took me to see what damage had been caused to Mr Miller's home. The front part of the house was in ruins. "The wall at the front of the house had fallen down and his bed, wardrobe etc were hanging at an angle (where the upstairs floor boards had given way and appeared to be about to fall into his front garden). The shops opposite, namely the chip shop, the Co-op Grocers, Co-op Butchers and Webb's Newsagents had damage to windows."

Empire Theatre and shops in Pinstone Street

Offices and shops in Church Street

CHAPTER EIGHT
Holocaust on The Moor

Atkinsons after the Blitz

The face of Sheffield city centre totally changed after the first night of the Blitz. Nowhere was that more apparent than The Moor. The busy shopping street was all but flattened. It rose again as stores were eventually rebuilt but monolithic sixties concrete was in vogue and it is only now, years later, that a multi-million pound regeneration will look to restore the architectural soul that was somehow lost in December 1940 when household names like Redgates, Atkinsons, Robert Brothers and others were flattened.

Marion Chapman said: "I was working down the bottom of The Moor on Broomhall Street at a laundry. The sirens had gone off and I walked down Hanover Street and someone shouts: 'Get down on the floor', as incendiary bombs were falling. Me and another lady from work ended up staying in the nearby cobbler's air raid shelter all night. An ARP man took us there. It was very crowded.

"By the time I got to the bottom of Ecclesall Road I could see all The Moor. You were being guided around the back. Marples was just rubble. We walked on the side of the road and passed what used to be the City Stores and water was gushing out. We managed to get to the Wicker towards Pitsmoor where I lived.

"At the time I was eighteen and I wanted a fox fur. I noticed the furriers down The Moor was all lit and on fire. My mum always used to say: 'If they'd have known about this they'd have given you one last week!'

"It was just one complete blaze all the way down The Moor. It was an experience I'll never forget. Wherever you looked there was fires and bangs."

Peter Hallam said: "Originally we got bombed out of Westbridge Street just off Staniforth Road.

"The front of the houses were knocked out. So my mother and me moved across to an empty shop which belonged to a relation on Milton Street which ran more or less parallel with The Moor.

"On the night of the bombing I remember crawling through the cellars and people were still singing upstairs at the pub. We walked from there to another relation at Wisewood.

"I remember walking down The Moor on the day after and there was little more than rubble, there was only a couple of places that were left standing.

"From there we saw all the changes as Marks & Spencer moved into the Locarno building and bombed out businesses took over other premises."

Mary Atkin, 92-years-old, said: "We were in a house set at the back of Lavers wood yard near Bramall Lane which was one of the first things that set on fire. We were only a few yards away. I'd never told my mum where I was going as I'd never expected there to be a full raid that night. We were settling down to our tea when we heard the sirens going and we thought that we better get in the Anderson Shelter. There was grass over it. I think they'd had made it as pretty as they could. All these bombs were coming down into this backyard and one I think blew a door off.

"There were by now a lot of people coming into the shelter. One lady came in with a baby and she was crying. I was nearest the doorway and someone shouted: 'Mary, can you go and fetch the door which has blown off'.

"To this day I don't know why I ran out to get it. I could hear the bombs whistling down and I raced back again. It must have been about seven o clock when we were in the shelter.

"You could hear all the noises of the houses being hit and the glass coming out. After around two hours a great big land mine came down on the other side of the road and five houses were down to the ground - we were blessed lucky.

"When the air raid sirens went again to signal the all clear we set off back about half past four in the morning. We got just onto the beginning of London Road where you could see The Moor - we were coming up John Street. There were a few trams on fire and it was freezing cold. As the firemen were squirting water on all these buildings it was freezing and they had to help us from slipping around.

"When we got to the bottom of Ecclesall Road we could tell The Moor had had it really bad. I remember Atkinsons had gone down straight away and there was also a big old Methodist Church at

Looking down The Moor

the bottom of Ecclesall Road, it was very big with columns, that went.

"There was a shop just round the corner from Ecclesall Road called Wainwrights, it was a men's shop; that was down. I think the corner sweetshop was down. There was a big shop at the other side that was called The Trimming House. Everybody went there. You could buy veils, dress materials and anything for a wedding. It was bombed.

"Even the bottom of Ecclesall Road had caught it. But the white tiled building on the bottom, the Co-op which had an arcade, luckily enough that was never bombed. We always said it was a shame that was demolished years later.

"We lived on Sharrowvale Road and mother had had an incendiary come through the corner of a ceiling. Everyone was huddled in a cellar. I think there were five houses connected and only one had a cellar that had been strengthened so everyone was in there. By the time you got in there it was very cramped.

"They all welcomed me with open arms as they'd been terribly worried about me.

"On the 15th December, my 21st birthday, I was in an air raid shelter! I hardly got any cards. I got married a year later. Everything was rationed and everything was fun. Some people said it was the best wedding they'd ever been to!

Mary Atkin ended up working at Laycocks on Archer Road and did more than her bit for the war effort. She rose through the ranks to end up making parts for the Spitfire.

She worked hard and enjoyed the job but like many of the city's 'Women of Steel' that kept armament production going whilst the men folk went overseas to fight, there was a unceremonious departure from her job.

She said: "When the war ended up I said to my colleagues - 'I bet we get sacked soon'. And lo and behold, the next day they finished us. And I said: 'Can't we stop on, we enjoy it?' And the boss said: 'No, because we're not doing them anymore.'

Mary Atkin on her wedding day

Looking up The Moor

Atkinsons, a total ruin

Walsh's burnt out store

The King and Queen talking to bombed out citizens

Looking up King Street

Williams Deacons Bank, Roberts Bros Ltd and other shops on The Moor

Central Cinema and shops and stores on The Moor

CHAPTER NINE
Dead bodies in Millhouses Park

Betty Hudson, 92-years-old, was sat in the Hippodrome with her husband when the raid was announced from the stage. She ended up walking to Totley after the all clear. Her father was in the police reserves. He saw a sight he'd never forget, dead bodies in Millhouses Park.

She said: "Me and my husband worked on West Street and we both had the same half day off. We always used to go to the cinema before we went home. Whilst we were watching the film there were two warnings. The picture stopped and someone came on the stage and said: 'There has been a warning. If anyone would like to go they can.' The second warning was when the incendiaries had started falling. One or two fires started around us.

"Well we were outside and we came to a little lane.

"We walked down this lane onto The Moor. It was full of fire engines, pipes all over the floor and water. All the buildings were ablaze. My husband's parents lived on Edmund Road so we made our way there, dashing in doorways as we heard bombs whistling down. We got there eventually and everyone was in the shelter.

"We hadn't been in there long when there was a bang on the shelter. We opened the door and a boy jumped in on us. He was absolutely terrified.

"He was a friend of my husband and he lived nearby. He'd come home and his house was gone.

"He'd no idea what had happened to his parents. I've never seen anyone that terrified in my life.

"The bombs were coming down all over. You could hardly miss them.

"By the time it was light and things had quietened down we came out the shelter. I began walking home towards Totley. We had some tea and sandwiches with my mum. We decided to come back into town to see what had happened. We got as far as Beauchief and you couldn't get any further down Millhouses. There were loads of unexploded bombs - ones we'd walked past hours earlier!

"My father was a police war reserve and when he came home he was shattered and he said: 'There are dead bodies all over Millhouses Park'.

"We got back onto West Street and the places we worked were okay but every time we saw someone we knew they'd cling onto us and say: 'Thank god you're safe, thank god you're here'. It was very emotional.

"It was a case of getting on as best we could."

A tram torn in two on the Wicker

First Aid party on parade

Below
A direct hit on Messrs. Walker & Hall's building

ARP Nurses

The ambulance workers saved countless lives

CHAPTER TEN
A whole community wiped out

Shirley Smith, now 77-years-old, was living with her family on the site of one of the biggest losses of life in the Sheffield Blitz. The lush inner city park, these days known as Devonshire Green, was, up until the bombings, a thriving, working class community.

Her house,187a West Street, which sits between West Street and Devonshire Street, is one of the few houses in the area that survived.

The damage to the dwelling, coupled with an unexploded bomb outside, left them with no alternative but to seek shelter with relatives in Attercliffe.

On December 15, 1940, they were bombed out for a second time and spent the next few weeks with hundreds of other homeless residents in High Storrs Rest Centre.

Shirley Smith said: "My grandfather had been visiting us. My mum went to take him to the tram stop on Ecclesall Road so he could get home. As she was coming past Moor Street she was told by the men that were on duty that there was a 'purple' [warning] on and that she better hurry up. The next thing was likely to be the sirens. She just got back to the top of Fitzwilliam Street where we lived when the first bomb dropped and she was virtually thrown into the house.

"At the time my father had made a bed down in the cellar which had been reinforced for all the people from the shops nearby. I had meant to have been sleeping down there ever since a raid a few weeks previous on St Philips Road. Mum came down and I was already there. My dad meanwhile was trying to get ready to go on duty to the ARP. He'd been shaving and his face was half lathered and every time he went to the top of the stairs to get finished

Much of the community around Devonshire Street was flattened

Total destruction on Campo Lane

another bomb dropped and he was knocked back down. This went on for literally hours and hours. We finally got out of the cellar at something like 5am the next morning and my dad was still, supposedly, trying to report for duty.

"The whole of Fitzwilliam Street was just one massive fire. I remember standing at the top of the steps and just seeing a mountain of broken down houses.

"My mum started to try and clear up as our windows were all smashed and our furniture was in the middle of Fitzwilliam Street and we were trying to salvage what we could. My mum was in the back yard and a policeman came and said: 'What

Bomb Disposal units work on Devonshire Street

on earth are you trying to do? There's a 500lb incendiary over the wall, you better get out'.

"So she got a few things together, my father came back and we walked with a couple of suitcases and flagged a car down and went to my uncles who had a shop on Attercliffe.

"We started off in the cellar with just four or five of us and ended up with 44 in there. When we came out the next morning their doors and windows were out and we'd been bombed out for a second time. We ended up going to High Storrs School.

"We were there for five or six weeks. My dad wasn't there so much as he was on ARP duty.

"High Storrs was full of people as nobody had anywhere to live. Everybody tried to help everyone else out by that stage. It was a time when people were used to living in tiny accommodation.

"We were supposed to have been going to the Central Picture House on The Moor on the first night of the Sheffield Blitz, to see Shirley Temple in *Bluebird,* but because of ARP duties we went on the Tuesday, otherwise we would have been in the place when it was hit.

"There were people that lived in a house on the corner near us on Fitzwilliam Street that were machine gunned as they tried to get to shelters across the road.

"Around the corner there was a jewellers shop that was kept by two old ladies. They tried to get out and they were found dead in the entrance. For a long time after I heard stories of people going down Division Street and picking up a gold rings and things.

"It was all back to back houses around Fitzwilliam Street and many of these had direct hits. There were only a couple left. I heard there were nearly 300 people killed in that area. We were very lucky.

"Kids take things in their stride I suppose. I remember being taught that if I heard a whistling to just lay on the floor and put your thumb in your mouth so the explosion wouldn't draw the breath out of you. "

Wings For Victory artwork painted by Shirley Smith's father

Popular Fitzwilliam Street wartime pub, The Raven

Total devastation in the Campo Lane area

Devastation at Brookhill

Blitzed shops on The Moor

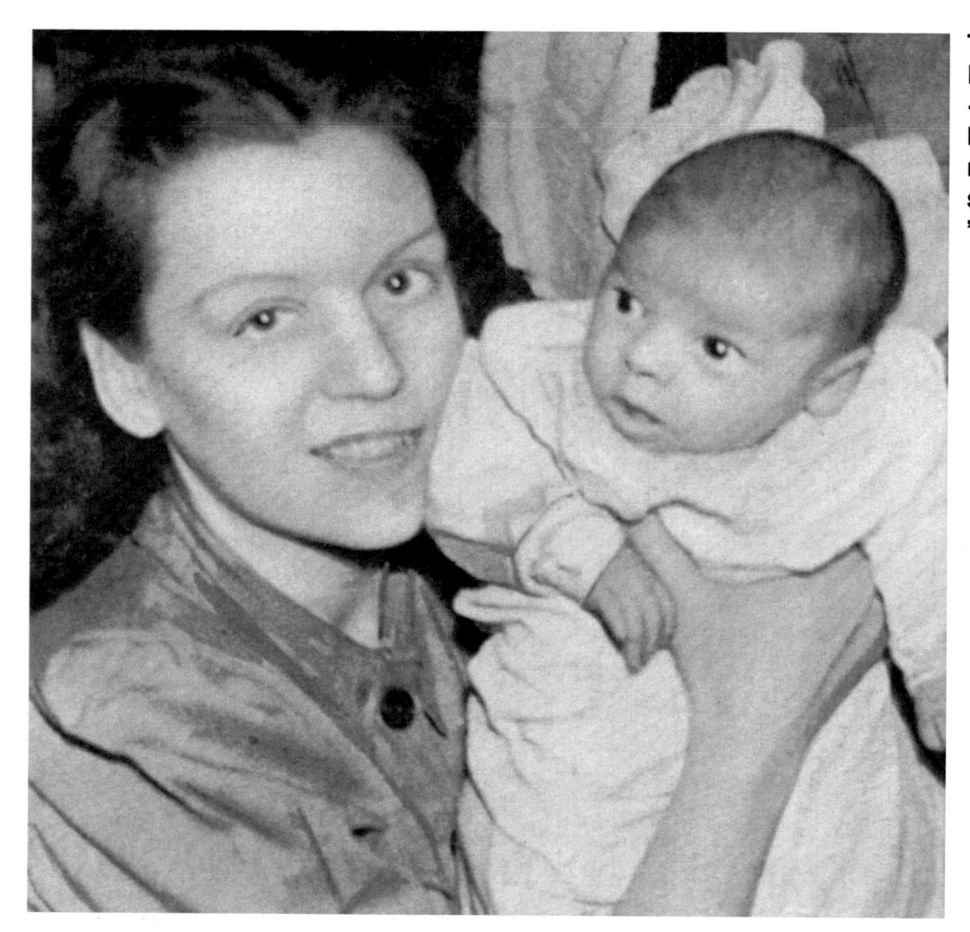

The baby born during the Blitz at Nether Edge Hospital - nurses made a barricade of beds to protect him and his mother, Mrs E. O'Brien. His soldier father christened him 'Blitz'

Shirley Smith's house, top right, is one of the few to remain to this day

CHAPTER ELEVEN
Remembering the lost ARP of Coleford Road

District Bank - Church Street

William Cooper lost his dad in one of the most tragic events of the Sheffield Blitz. He died, along with several colleagues, when the ARP station they were manning on Coleford Road was hit.

He said: "September 3rd, 1939. Time 11.15am, a bright and sunny Sunday morning. Neville Chamberlain, our Prime Minister had just been on the radio to announce that he had issued an ultimatum to Germany to withdraw their troops from Poland, and that should Hitler fail to submit such an undertaking, England would declare war. No such undertaking was given, so for the second time in just over twenty years, our country was at war with Germany. I remember standing with my father at the bottom of our passage, basking in the Autumn sunshine. All at once the eerie sound of the air raid siren was heard. We expected bombs to rain down on us immediately, but life went on just as before. Our family used to like Sunday for the simple reason that the radio series 'Hippodrome' was broadcast on Sunday night. Its main characters were Harry Korris and Enoch, who played the stooge. An air raid shelter had been delivered to our humble home, and had been erected in our back garden. My father planted mushrooms at the back of the shelter, of which he was very proud. My eldest sister, who was named Gladys, and my elder brother Robert used to volunteer to clean the shelter out after it had rained, as the water used to settle on the shelter floor.

"There was another reason that they were so

keen, and that was that they had both started to smoke. Eventually my father found out about this and caught them. He pulled both of them out of the shelter and made them smoke a cigarette each. After smoking about half of it, their complexions turned a funny grey. For the moment both smokers decided that it was bad for their health in more ways than one.

"My father was a labourer at Kayser Ellison's steel works which was about a mile from where we lived.

Sheffield ATC cadets at Stephenson Hall

"During the next few months, we went through what was called the Phoney War. The Germans mounted a few nuisance raids and we did the same. At this moment in time the war was not going very well for us and the miracle of Dunkirk had just been accomplished. After this, the raids began to be more frequent and mostly at night.

"My father, Robert Cooper, who had been injured in a steelworks, joined the ARP as a warden. He would come home from work, have his tea, don his ARP overall and helmet and report to the local ARP post for duty.

"When my father came off duty he would tell us what state of alert the town was in.

"The highest state of alert was the purple. When he told my mother that the purple was on, she would gather us all together and we would sleep in the shelter. This went on, on a regular basis until my father put his foot down. He said that we might as well get killed by a bomb as die from pneumonia in a damp shelter. My youngest brother John, was only six months old at the time. When the Ack-ack guns had been firing at passing raiders, my friends and I used to go round the roads looking for shrapnel from the spent Ack-ack shells.

"My father gave his life during the Sunday night Blitz, along with nine of his comrades; they did not find his body for a week.

"Our home had been completely destroyed and we were living with our Aunt Ada, my father's sister.

"They brought my father's body there for burial. It was screwed down with orders that it was to remain that way, but my mother had other ideas.

"She wanted to say her goodbyes and to see who she was burying.

"Waiting while we were all in bed, she unscrewed the coffin lid and took her last look at my father's body. His body was so badly damaged that she could only identify him from his clothing.

"At the time of the Sunday night blitz, my father was working. As soon as the sirens went, he came home in his working clothes. He always wore a waistcoat. Somehow or other, my mother got hold of this waistcoat, and she treasured that piece of clothing for thirty years, until she was persuaded to throw it away.

"The bizarre thing about the waistcoat was that you could still see the bloodstains after all that time. With my father gone, my mother had the task of bringing up six children. A few months after my mother's sister Nellie died in childbirth, leaving two young children, which my mother, Annie Cooper, added to her own brood, therefore bringing up eight children in all.

"By this time my sister Gladys and brother Robert were of working age, but at the time of my father's funeral, there was no state benefit. Through his kind generosity, my Uncle Cedric, paid all expenses for the funeral and our funeral clothes."

Lost to a land mine in Parson Cross

79-year-old Greta Philips lost her aunt, uncle and three cousins to a land mine in Parson Cross. Her father was left unemployed after the first night of the Sheffield Blitz.

Greta Philips said: "My father was the manager of the Home & Colonial - the equivalent of Tesco and Asda now. It was a food shop on Castle Street where the Co-op is now. I can remember going down with him and all that was left was a big hole. In it was a safe and he had to open it and take all the frazzled money out and take it to the police station.

"He was then left without a job. He was called up for the navy - I remember my mother being dressed in a voluminous white nightie, opening the letter saying he'd been called up.

"My aunt, uncle and three cousins were killed

at Parson Cross by a land mine. The family had just moved into the house. Whilst the furniture was being moved in, she had a premonition that something awful was going to happen there. Their eldest son was a at a dance at Sheffield City Hall and he got home to find his family gone. He joined the navy and is now 90.

"When I was 8, in 1940, I was chosen as the May Queen at school - I was Lilac Queen. I still think that the reason I was made May Queen was because all the other kids at school had fathers who were in munitions factories and mine was in the navy.

"Whenever my father came home on leave he would never go to the shelter in the garden. He and my mother never went in our shelter - we would go in our neighbours' shelter. How we got everyone in I don't know. I wouldn't go in without my white Persian cat, Peggy.

"I remember my mum taking me to town to see Guy Gibson, the famous pilot who had bombed dams in Germany as the leader of the Dam Busters. His car pulled up outside what is now HL Brown Jewellers. He got out, he was a very handsome man.

"After his release from the war, my father brought home his demob suit and his sailor suit. He lit a bonfire in the garden and burnt them."

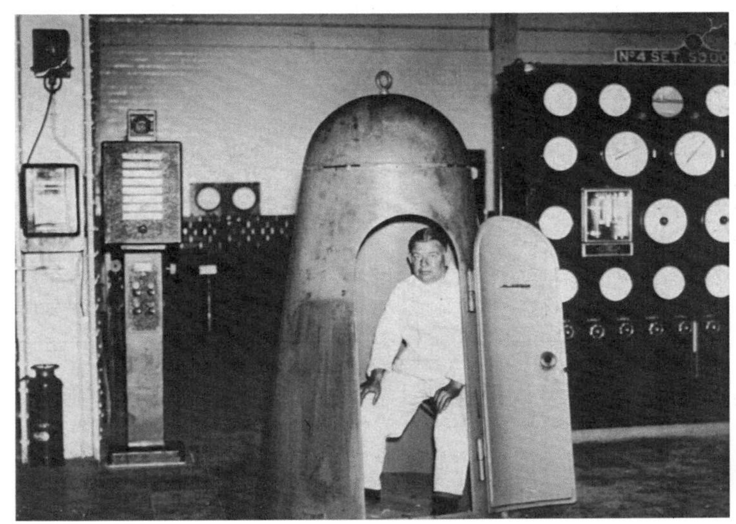

Special shelters were provided for essential staff at Sheffield's Blackburn Meadows Power Station

Memorial service held on the site of the Coleford Road Warden's Post in December 1941 - a year after the loss of ten lives on the site

Many churches were in ruins including these - St Mark's Church in Broomhill (top) and Burngreave Road Methodist Church

CHAPTER TWELVE

Central Library co-ordinates the relief effort

Ninety two year-old Joyce Spurr spent the first night of the Sheffield Blitz in the Library Theatre, under Central Library. She didn't realise, until the following morning, just how lucky they'd been - a huge crater containing an unexploded bomb was on the junction of Surrey Street and Tudor Street, just yards away from the library.

Just how the city's bombed out population would have fared if the bomb had gone off we'll never know; the library spent the following day (and weeks after) helping co-ordinate the relief effort via its information service, which had been geared to assisting such an event.

Joyce Spurr is one of the last surviving library staff who was part of that relief effort seven decades ago.

She said: "I was working in the Reference Library as a junior assistant, when the alarm sounded at about 7.30pm (we closed at 9pm in those days).

"We were always expecting something to happen as it had been happening in London and places like that.

"We led the public down to the Library Theatre, which was sandbagged as an official shelter. It was absolutely full but people still kept coming in. Me and one of the janitors had to keep going upstairs to make sure that no incendiary bombs had taken hold on the upper floors. There were frightening crashes and bangs, and the building shook. Some of the noise was from anti-aircraft guns. The sky outside was red from fires of the burning buildings.

"During the evening, some people came in covered in dust and debris. They had come from the evening classes in the College of Art in Arundel Street nearby. It had received a direct hit from a shell and was completely demolished, which was a great pity as it had been an ornate Victorian building with classical sculptures on the facade.

"When the 'all clear' sounded, and we came out,the Air Raid Wardens directed us round a huge crater in which was an unexploded bomb. It was at the corner of Surrey Street and Tudor Street, just alongside the corner of the library, so we had a lucky escape.

Joyce Spurr - she directed the bombed out population arriving at Central Library desperate for help

"I had to walk home to Woodseats. When I saw The Moor, I was appalled, as it was a blazing inferno with the black skeletons of trams silhouetted against the flames. There were lumps of debris and cables hanging down. It made such a vivid impression on me that the image remained with me for the rest of my life.

"I passed over fires and saw a notably huge one at Laver's Timber Yard on Queen's Road.

"I remember wondering if I'd have any parents and any house when I got home. Fortunately they'd not been hit.

"My parents were of, course, relieved to see me, but I knew I had to be back at work by 8am, so I only had two hours rest on the settee before walking back to the library. There were no trams or buses of course. The buses started to appear several days later.

"There were still a lot of flames coming out of buildings on The Moor the following day.

"The library had become a gigantic information bureau - I was very impressed about how well organised they were. Representatives of different parts of the Town Hall sat at desks in the Reference Library to deal with problems of people who had been bombed out and had nowhere to live, or no gas, electricity or water supply, or needed roofs repairing. Desks had little flags on telling people which issue they could sort out, whether it be no gas, bombed out or whatever.

"Instead of people having to trail round the Town Hall, it was all there at once. The Central Library was the city's information service.

"But it was quite distressing the next morning as people were coming in. In fact an acquaintance of mine came in whilst I had the job of directing everyone. He said: "My wife and son have just been killed - the house got a direct hit". He'd got no home, no family and nowhere to go. There must have been lots of stories like that.

"I do remember how in control everybody seem to be. I only remember one woman who was moaning and crying and wasn't in control. Somebody said: 'I've got some brandy, I'll give her a tot'. She was a bit better after that. People were quite calm generally. I suppose it was because we were expecting the attacks and we thought: 'We're not going to let those damn Germans get us down'. We were proud of our steel industry, our cutlery and everything else Sheffield was unique in the world for then.

"The Newspaper Room and Children's Library were receiving people who had been bombed out, and the staff kitchen was serving tea, soup and sandwiches to them all day. The police took over the Cataloguing Department and the Library staff compiled records of the missing and dead people as the information came in. My job was to divert people to the appropriate place for their problems.

"I think this operation went on at least two or three weeks. I also remember it was very cold weather and I had chilblains all over my fingers and I ended up having to have them bandaged up.

"It had been well planned and organised to come into operation immediately and credit, for a large part, must go to the City Librarian, Mr J.P. Lamb.

"It's an experience I'll never forget."

Joyce Spurr painted the shocking sight of The Moor on the night of December 12/13, 1940

Corner of Bank Street after the night of hell on December 12/13 1940

What was left of Moorhead

The Wicker suffered substantial damage - you can still see clearly see a patched up hole in the Wicker Arches to this day

Shops at Moorhead

CHAPTER THIRTEEN
Margaret's Christmas present survives the Blitz

Margaret Emery was taken to see the glittering yuletide displays at Walsh's department store in early December 1940. Despite the war, parents did their utmost to ensure some kind of normality for their children and they always strived to make Christmas special, however bad things were. She met Santa and ordered her present for the big day.

Many struggled to find festive cheer that year. Christmas Day landed less than two weeks after the Sheffield Blitz. Thousands were in rest shelters or staying in cramped conditions with friends and neighbours. Many had their Christmas dinner in Sheffield City Hall which opened its doors as a communal feeding station, something that carried on throughout the war.

Margaret Emery was one of the lucky ones. Despite Walsh's being completely destroyed, her Christmas present survived.

She said: "Just a few days before the Blitz I had been taken to Walsh's store to see Father Christmas and order a doll's cot for my Christmas present. During the Blitz the store was burnt to the ground. Dad, who was home on leave, went to Walsh's to see what had happened to my present.

"He was told all the childrens' toys were stored in a warehouse a few streets from the main store and had survived the bombing. The Walsh's family home was the Mount at Broomhill, part of which was converted into a store so the business could carry on.

"We lived in a cul de sac with approx ten houses on each side of the road. Every alternate house had its cellar strengthened and trap doors lead through into the adjoining cellars so it was possible to go the full length of the road from one cellar to another. During the Blitz, mum didn't like the idea of being trapped in the cellar if the house collapsed so we all went up to the living room. Dad was home on leave and making tea in front of the living room window when a bomb landed nearby, blowing the windows in. Fortunately for him the windows were covered with plywood boards, which withstood the blast and saved him from the flying glass.

"At Easter time during the war, mum made Easter eggs from soya flour and covered them with a cocoa based chocolate. Delicious!

"At Christmas time we made presents of flowers from sealing wax and twigs.

"We went to a large house on Fulwood Road to collect our gas masks. Each child was given a sweet along with its mask. We took our gas masks to school and at one time we took sandwiches to school , we had a shorter lunch time so that school could finish at 2 o'clock, as it was feared the attacks would begin earlier.

"In an effort to make things go further, the cinders and ashes from the previous night's fire in the Yorkshire range would be riddled to separate the ash from the cinders, which could be used again."

This girl is delighted to find her teddy in the ruins of her house

The bizarre sight of half-furnished rooms exposed to the elements became commonplace

Sheffield picked itself up, dusted itself down and Churchill held up its resilience as an example to the whole nation.

Here's a church (right) that was used to store stock from a large, blitzed store.

Stores sprung up everywhere - here's one in a cinema (below)

Munitions and other workers from Sheffield spent their holidays in Derbyshire in August 1941

Surviving the Blitz in Shiregreen

CHAPTER FOURTEEN

The bank that liked to say no

Charles and Ada Ward of 22 Skye-Edge Road were bombed out of their home on the second night of the Sheffield Blitz, December 15, 1940. Theirs was the only house on the road to be hit.

Despite being completely gutted, having no roof and little remaining bar four walls, the mortgage bills kept coming.

With no home and no belongings, the situation was further compounded by the unrelenting attitude of the Halifax Building Society who kept up demands for payments arising from the uninhabitable shell.

It took nearly eight years for their house to be rebuilt. Charles and Ada's story wasn't that unusual.

HARRY GLASS, LL.M.,
Solicitor.
TELEPHONE 21856

36 & 38, Bank Street,
Sheffield, 1.

HG/JB

19th August 1941

Dear Sir,

Halifax Building Society.
Property 22 Skye Edge Road, Sheffield.

The Halifax Building Society have asked me to write to you with regard to your Mortgage Account in respect of the above property. I understand that this property was destroyed by enemy action in December last and whilst I sympathise with you in the loss you have sustained, your obligations to the Society for the mortgage debt and interest still continue. Inaccordance with the general practice of the Society in cases of this kind they are prepared to give every assistance to their Borrowers but they expect that they will receive some co-operation from them in meeting their obligations. They have proposed in your case to apply only for interest on the mortgage which is £1/5/11 per lunar month and on this basis of dealing with the matter arrears have now accumulated to the extent of £9/1/5.

As you have paid nothing at all on your Mortgage Account this year I trust you will be good enough to make satisfactory arrangements with me and let me have a substantial payment by the end of this week.

Yours faithfully,

H. Glass

Mr. C.A. Ward,
31 City Road,
Sheffield.

31, City Road,
Sheffield.

July 25th. 1942.

Sirs,

I beg to bring to your notice the predicament I am in with reference to my House which was destroyed absolutely in the December 1939 raids on Sheffield.

The House destroyed was situated at 22 Skyedge Road, Sheffield, and was levelled on Sunday, December 15th. 1939, destroying everything we had.

I was purchasing same through the "Halifax Building Society" Roll No. 521215, now this Company is pressing me very much to continue payments, but I do not see why they should do as I have not got the House.

Original Mortgage £375, Society now say Debt is over £380. Have put in claim £400 for Furniture etc., but have as yet not received anything at all. Corporation have refused to do anything until after the War.

I would like if you can to send a Representative to see the site with a view to obtaining a license to build. I have consulted a local Solicitor, but I am unable to get any satisfaction.

Yours truly,

War Damage Commision,
36, York Place,
Leeds.

31, City Road
Sheffield 2
13th April. 42.

Sir,

Could you please inform me, whether The Halifax Building Society can claim for the interest on my house of 22, Skye-Edge Road? as there are only the four walls left, it being completely burnt out, and everything we possessed, lost, during the night raid December 14th–16th 1940.

So far, the interest has accumulated to £26. and we are not in a position to pay the equivalent of two rents; but are only too willing to go back into the house if rebuilt. (this being the only one on the estate).

Would you kindly inform me as early as possible?

Yours Sincerely.
Ada Ward. (Mrs.)

ESTABLISHED 1853 INCORPORATED 1875

HALIFAX BUILDING SOCIETY.

TELEPHONE No. 22897.

DISTRICT MANAGER: M. H. DENHAM.

49, 51, 53 & 55, SURREY STREET, SHEFFIELD.

PHS/T. 12th November, 1941.

C. A. Ward Esq.,
31, City Road,
SHEFFIELD. 2.

Dear Sir,

Roll No. A.521215.

I do not appear to have heard from you in response to my letter of the 7th November, and I shall be glad if you will advise me whether you are now able to make some payment on this account each month.

The Directors have assisted you as far as possible by suspending the subscription subject to payment of interest only, and I should like to have your co-operation in the matter.

Yours faithfully,

M. H. Denham

District Manager.

Front Room

	£	s.	d
1 Three piece suite	18	18	0
1 Secretaire	12	19	6
1 Lamp stand	1	0	0
1 Carpet x	4	4	0
1 Rug	1	10	0
1 Gramophone (Console)	12	12	0
Records			
1 Bookcase	7	7	0
2 Chairs approx Books	2	0	0
Cushions 5 6/6	1	12	6
Contents of secretaire			
1 doz glasses 7/- 1 Wine 7/-			
10/6 ½ doz Tumblers 1/6 1 [illegible] HW Jug & Tum. 4/-			
Socks etc 1 doz [illegible] 9/-		9	0
Ties, collars etc			
Books Encyclopedia etc 30/-			
E. light fittings	1	10	0
Vacuum cleaner	3	0	0
Easiwork Cooker	5	0	0
Curtains Runners etc	2	10	0
1 Clock	1	0	0
Glass vases approx	3	0	0
Mirror	1	10	0
Chrome Basket		10	0
[illegible]		15	0
Ash Tray		7	6
Pictures			

WAR DAMAGE ACT 1943 (PART II) - PRIVATE CHATTELS SCHEME

A Payable Order (the yellow card) is enclosed in settlement of the War Damage Private Chattels claim of which particulars are given on the Order. From the amount of the assessment, advance payments (if any) made by the Assistance Board, Customs and Excise Department, Board of Trade, or Local Authorities have been deducted; and where the damage occurred before 1st May, 1941, on which date the Private Chattels Scheme came into force, the amount chargeable in lieu of insurance premium has been deducted as follows:—

Nil on first £300 of the assessment;
1% on the next £1,700;
1½% on the next £1,000;
2% on the next £7,000.

The Payable Order may be passed through a bank or paid into an account in the Post Office Savings Bank, a Trustee Savings Bank, or the Birmingham Municipal Savings Bank. It cannot be **cashed** at a Post Office.

If you have no bank account, payment may be obtained through a third person (for example, a friend or tradesman) who is willing to pass the Payable Order through his bank for you.

Your particular attention is called to the enclosed Government leaflet about investment in National Savings.

A statement is also enclosed (the pink card) showing the amount of income tax that has been deducted from the interest. This statement will enable those claimants who are not liable to tax at the standard rate to apply to their Tax Officer for a refund of the tax, in whole or in part.

Supplementary payments are made only in respect of claims assessed at more than £25 and less than £1,200 for war damage which occurred before the end of 1941, where the claims were not wholly paid up by the end of that year. Supplementary payments are calculated on the amount of the assessment as follows:—

Assessments exceeding £25 but not exceeding £350 - 50 per cent of the assessment
Assessments exceeding £350 but not exceeding £762/10/0 - a flat increase of £175
Assessments exceeding £762/10/0 but not exceeding £1,200 - two-fifths of the difference between the assessment and £1,200

It is not necessary to acknowledge the receipt of the Payable Order.

Issued by THE BOARD OF TRADE (OP/1)
JERSEY ROAD, OSTERLEY, ISLEWORTH, MIDDLESEX

ALACRA BUSINESS FORMS TP

PAYABLE ORDER No. Z 271450

The Standard Rate in the £ of Tax that has been deducted is:—	S.	D.
	9	0

BOARD OF TRADE

The final amount payable as shown on the Payable Order is arrived at as follows:—

£	S.	D.	
270.	9.	0	AMOUNT OF ASSESSMENT OUTSTANDING.
44.	9.	6	ADD INTEREST ON ABOVE AMOUNT (IT IS NOT PAYABLE ON ADVANCES), AT 2½% PER ANNUM FROM DATE OF DAMAGE TO DATE OF PAYABLE ORDER.
20.	0.	3	DEDUCT INCOME TAX ON THE INTEREST AT THE CURRENT STANDARD RATE.
175.	0.	0	ADD SUPPLEMENTARY PAYMENT (IF ANY).
£ 469.	18.	3	NET AMOUNT PAYABLE.

3. PC. balance Pre Act.

WAR DAMAGE ACT, 1941 (Part II)

PRIVATE CHATTELS

INSURANCE & COMPANIES DEPARTMENT,
BOARD OF TRADE, ROMNEY HOUSE, EAST,
TUFTON STREET, LONDON, S.W.1.

Ref. PCS. R. 7398. Date 9.10.42

Claimant Charles A. Ward.

For loss at 22, Skye Edge Road. Sheffield. on the 15.12.40

£ 355 : - : -	Assessed amount of damage.
£ 84 : - : -	Granted for distress or hardship.
£ : 11 : -	Premium deducted.
£ 270 : 9 : - d	Balance deferred.

SIR/MADAM,

I am directed by the Board of Trade to inform you that the sum described above as balance deferred is the amount payable by them in respect of the above loss. Payment of the balance will be deferred and interest at the rate of 2½ per cent. per annum will accrue on the balance from the occurrence of the damage until such time as payment is made.

A deduction from the amount of your claim as assessed has been made in lieu of insurance premium on the basis shown below. STET

You are requested to sign and return the attached form of acceptance.

I am, Sir/Madam,
Your obedient Servant,
GERSHOM W. DAVIS.

1 per cent. on the first £2,000.
1½ " " next £1,000.
2 " " " £7,000.

[81647] 28666/8242 9/41 745/3

TELEPHONE Nº 22997 SHEFFIELD. ESTABLISHED 1853. INCORPORATED 1873

Halifax Building Society.

OFFICE HOURS.
9-30 TO 4 DAILY.
9-0 TO 12 THURSDAYS.
6-0 TO 8 FRIDAY EVENINGS.

SHEFFIELD BRANCH OFFICE. 19/55, Surrey Street.

DISTRICT MANAGER,
M. H. DENHAM.

REFERENCE SG/T.

Sheffield, 1 31st March, 1944.

C. A. Ward Esq.,
31, City Road,
Sheffield.

Dear Sir,

Roll No. A. 521215.
War Damage Concession in Interest Charges.

You may have observed the recent Press announcement that the Directors have decided to make an important concession in interest charges to certain mortgagor members of the Society whose properties have, by enemy action, either been destroyed or so seriously damaged as to make the properties uninhabitable for a period of six months or more.

According to the Society's records, you qualify for this concession by way of a reduction in the rate of interest in your account to 2½% from the 12th December, 1940. to the 31st January, 1944. The amount to which you are entitled is £ 24. 10. 5d. and this sum is being credited to your account in reduction of the amount owing at the 1st February, 1944. If you will kindly let me have your passbook at your convenience I will have the appropriate entry made therein.

In the case of properties which are completely destroyed or which are still not fit for habitation in consequence of war damage, it is proposed to continue the concession until further notice.

I hope this practical expression of the consideration which the Directors have decided you should have, in view of your most unfortunate experience, will be of assistance to you and I have to assure you of the Society's desire to afford you through its District Managers and Agents, any help

- 1 - p.t.o.

BOARD OF TRADE 14th. JULY 1947

WAR DAMAGE ACT (PRIVATE CHATTELS SCHEME)

STATEMENT OF INTEREST PAID AND INCOME TAX DEDUCTED ON SETTLEMENT OF WAR DAMAGE PRIVATE CHATTELS CLAIM

ORDER NO.	FILE REF.	NAME
271450	R---7398	WARD-CA---------------

GROSS INTEREST £	s	d	TAX DEDUCTED £	s	d
--44	-9	-6	-20	--	-3

INCOME TAX AT THE STANDARD RATE IN FORCE ON THE ABOVE DATE HAS BEEN DEDUCTED FROM THE GROSS INTEREST ON THE AMOUNT OUTSTANDING. IF YOU ARE ENTITLED TO ANY REDUCTION OF TAX YOU SHOULD WRITE TO YOUR TAX OFFICE ENCLOSING THIS FORM AND QUOTING YOUR INCOME TAX REFERENCE IF KNOWN

POWERS-SAMAS ACCOUNTING MACHINES TRADE MARK POWERS SFP.2695

PAT. NO. 398223 REG. NO. 771461

"It used to frighten me to bloody death when those sirens went"

Betty Flanagan (nee Sheldon) was ten-years-old when war broke out. She was living in Shiregreen.

She said: "We practically seemed to live in the shelter. I remember one night we heard all the bombs dropping and the next day my mother took me up town. I remember Marples was flattened to the ground.

"It used to frighten me to death when those bloody sirens went. You could hear the bombs whistling overhead and you think: 'where's that going to go'.

The man who later became her husband, Eddie Flanagan, was 14-years-old when war broke out and also living in Shiregreen. He remembers the Blitz vividly.

He said: "We were in Glossop Road Baths on the night of the Blitz. We used to go every week swimming. We had to walk it back from there to Shiregreen as all the trams were on fire. It was a right mess in the middle of town. We walked back through it after the all clear went. We passed through where Marples had been, that was awful.

"All round Fitzalan Square was bombed. We walked down to the Wicker Arches and all round there was hit.

"We walked up through Pitsmoor and they'd bombed all the way."

Eddie Flanagan joined the army when he was 17.

He said: "I was part of the D Day landings. I went right through France, right through Belgium and I got as far as Holland. I was going across this building when a machine gunner hit me in the leg.

"As I went down he was still firing and I thought, if I stay here he's going to hit me again. I ran and collapsed in a farmyard and my best mate, a kid called David Fletcher, started bandaging me up. As he was bandaging me a sniper hit him and he died in my arms."

Eddie Flanagan was eventually taken to Brussels before being flown back to England.

Taking time out in Sheffield - precise area unknown

CHAPTER FIFTEEN
Wedding night in a cellar

Gladys Bunting (nee Couldwell) spent her wedding night in a cellar. But even the Luftwaffe couldn't stop her and her husband George enjoying 63 happy years together. Their daughter, Pamela Powell, was kind enough to submit her mother's memories of the Sheffield Blitz and the aftermath.

Gladys said: "It was December 12, 1940, and I was due to marry George on the 21st. He was working nights in the steelworks and I was preparing the small bedsit where we would live after we were married. It was in a house opposite the Catholic Church on Abbeydale Road. The sirens went and I continued cleaning. The owner of the house said I should leave and go to the cellar below the shops opposite. I was only 20-years-old and this was a bit daunting as I knew no one. It was cold and everyone was sitting on stone slabs, but a bus driver who had to abandon his bus went to fetch some seating to make it more bearable.

"Eventually the 'all clear' went and we made our way back outside and then we realised what had happened during the latest raid. However, that was nothing compared with what was waiting for me as I walked into town.

"As I walked along The Moor I realised just how much damage had been done. I saw burned out trams and demolished shops. I was suddenly grabbed by a stranger and pulled along. I turned round and a wall I had just passed crashed to the ground. I didn't know this man, but he saved my life.

"I then began to wonder if there had been any damage at the steelworks. I decided to continue my journey along The Moor in amongst the debris towards Davy's on Fargate where I worked in the bakery. I explained to my boss where I had been and told him I was going to walk to Crookes to check that my family was OK and that my wedding dress was still in one piece. I continued on foot as there was no transport, either trams or buses.

"From a distance I would see that some windows were blown out in our house, but to my relief all my family were well and my wedding dress unharmed.

"Of course, I needed to know if there was any damage to the works where George worked so I made my way to where he lived in Heeley (behind Ponsfords). When I arrived there his mother said that he had returned home from his shift work and after checking on his parents, had set off to find me.

Gladys and George on their wedding day

"We somehow passed each other in the confusion in the city centre. (Both of us on foot) He arrived at my home about the same time that I arrived at his.

"Fortunately, he had the sense to stay in Crookes knowing that I would eventually return. At least we knew that we were both safe.

"The wedding did go ahead, but without flowers, cake etc. and during the reception at George's parent's home the sirens went and all the guests moved into the cellar for our wedding night."

Table collapsed and killed them all

Gladys Garfitt lived on Edgar Street in Pitsmoor at the time of the Sheffield Blitz. She said: "I was nineteen when the war broke out. I went to work following the Blitz not knowing if I'd got a place to go to or not.

"When my future husband got home he found the house next door had been bombed. In his cellar he'd got a stone table. Next door, the couple with the two children had gone down into their cellar and gone under their table. It had collapsed and killed them all.

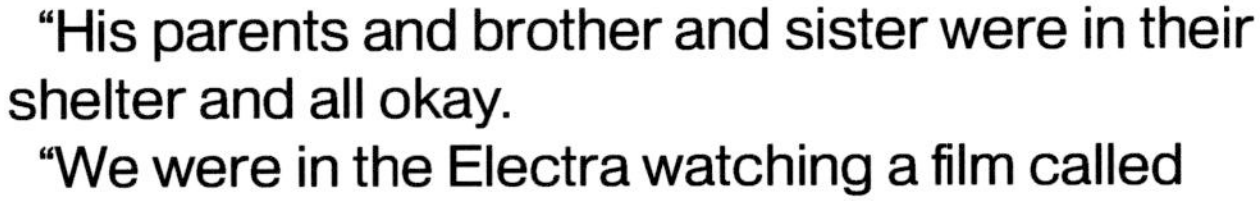

"His parents and brother and sister were in their shelter and all okay.

"We were in the Electra watching a film called *Green Hell* - it's fair to say we came out to a living hell. We sat in this nearby shelter with our feet in water. There was this little old lady and she'd brought her budgie in a cage. She was on her own but she wouldn't leave her budgie.

"We sat in there until the all clear sirens went. I got home in the middle of the night and got to bed at 5am. I was up again and 7am and had to walk through it to Arundel Street where I worked in a factory."

George Street Corner

Westminster Hotel and Bank and Mulberry Street

Though the shops survived - every window on High Street was smashed

Major damage on St Mary's Road

Even the Jessop Hospital for women was hit

Blitz damage to W T Flather Ltd

Destruction to Lavers timberworks on Bramall Lane

CHAPTER SIXTEEN

Emergency planning struggled to cope

Elaborate planning had been arranged to accommodate 10,000 bombed out Sheffielders if the worst happened and the city was badly hit. Another 1,600 volunteers had been enrolled and trained up and attached to rest centres and feeding stations.

But as the January 1941 edition of 'All Clear', the ARP newsletter, said, the service could not cope.

"...no scheme could have anticipated the ghastly setbacks which this service suffered.

"The headquarters of the organising body obtained three direct hits. Over 75 per cent of the centres had been rendered untenable... At one time over 23,000 persons were present in the temporary centres.

"Many members of the staff and of the voluntary personnel were themselves homeless - but they carried on."

What the service achieved was incredible considering the circumstances. Over 60,000 hot meals were distributed within 24 hours of the 'all clear' from one institution alone.

Within hours a host of alternative rest premises were secured including schoolrooms, church halls, clubs, picture houses and more.

Medical services were badly hit. Four of the largest hospitals in the city were damaged in the raids and large quantities of medical supplies destroyed.

Patients had be evacuated 'under fire' and operations continued throughout.

Mobile canteens appeared from Manchester, Leeds, Wakefield and Bradford to help feed the hungry alongside vehicles from the Church Army, the Salvation Army and others.

Hundreds of homes across the city opened their doors to the homeless.

'All Clear' said: "The spirit of Sheffield was clearly displayed by the numerous offers made to provide accommodation."

Women sorting and stacking clothes for distribution amongst the homeless

Furnival Street

High Court

Bottom of High Street

Foster's Stores, Waingate

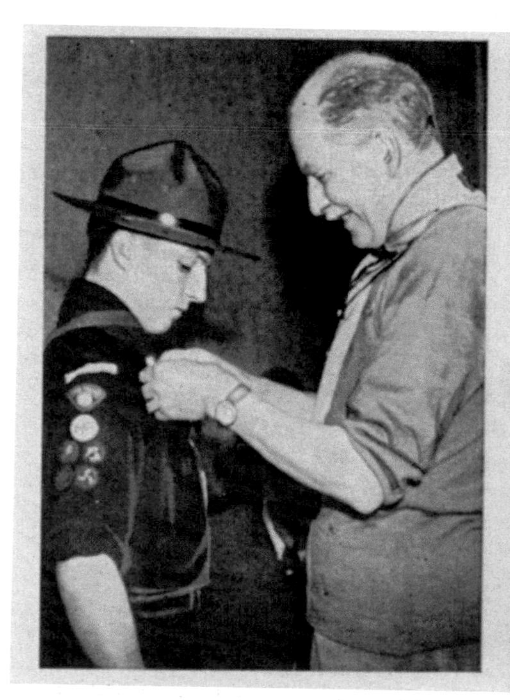

Air raid hero John Flinn, a 16-year-old boy scout, received the Gilt Cross for Gallantry for taking charge of a woman who had been rescued from a demolished home and wheeling her on a grocer's barrow to a first aid post. He wore a saucepan to protect himself from flying shrapnel

Prime Minister Winston Churchill pays a visit to a Sheffield steelworks just days before the Sheffield Blitz in November 1940

CHAPTER SEVENTEEN
Why Blitz Sheffield?

There have been numerous theories around the precise nature and reason for the bombings over the years. Why weren't the steel mills of the east end more badly damaged and why, if armaments were the target which was always the assumption, were bombs dropped miles away in virtually every suburb of the city? Dave Manvell has his own theory.

He said: "In Neil Anderson's excellent book, *Sheffield's Date with Hitler*, he points out that from available evidence and German aerial reconnaissance maps, the attack on Sheffield, by the Luftwaffe, was following a plan of strategic bombing. The aim being to target public and municipal buildings, also the city centre, the administrative and financial heart of the city, as well as industrial targets. Strategic bombing was designed to affect civilian life and destroy morale as well as industry and commerce.

"On the 12th of December, 1940, the suburbs and city centre sustained heavy damage with comparatively light damage to industry. The German pathfinders entered the city in a southerly direction flying down the valley to the east end, marking the targets with a mixture of incendiaries and parachute flares. Looking at the map plotting where the bombs fell it can be clearly seen that some of the pathfinders were following the LMS line from Millhouses to the east end. As the bombs clearly fell along its path it can be presumed that industrial targets were to be attacked.

"The German high command would have been well aware of Sheffield's industrial history, as German and Sheffield industrialists and metallurgists had been collaborating since Victorian times. In fact the Siemens method for steel making had been invented around 1856 by Sir William Siemens, a German who along with his brothers came to live in England in 1844. The fuses used in the British WW1 shells had been invented by German industrial giant Krupps, as was one of the hardening processes for armour plate. After WW1, bizarrely, royalties were paid to Krupps, for each fuse used. In the 1930s Vickers Works purchased a 15 ton steam powered drop hammer from Germany. In the early years of the war this was the only hammer in the country able to forge the crankshafts for the Rolls Royce Merlin engines which in turn powered the Spitfire fighter and Lancaster bomber. The Germans would also be aware of the large naval gun barrels and marine shafts produced in the cities steel works and other items of strategic importance such as railway lines, points and stainless steel products for marine applications to name but a few.

"Unable to bomb the east end on the first raid on the 12/13th, December, it looks clearly as though due to this failure they came back on the 15th of December to finish the attack.

"This time Attercliffe, Darnall Brightside and Tinsley, came in for a very heavy attack. Hitting the works of English Steel, Hadfields , Brown Bayleys and Steel Peach and Tozer the attack petering out just beyond Tinsley. Despite extensive damage to the works and civilians homes, the effect on industry and its war effort was surprisingly small."

The King and Queen stop to look at a baby carried by a bombed mother staying at Anns Road Rest Centre

Meersbrook youngsters prepare their VE Bonfire in May 1945 on Rushdale Avenue

Below
VE celebrations on Sanderson Road

VE Day celebrations in Barker's Pool

Churchill returns to receive the Freedom of the City in 1951

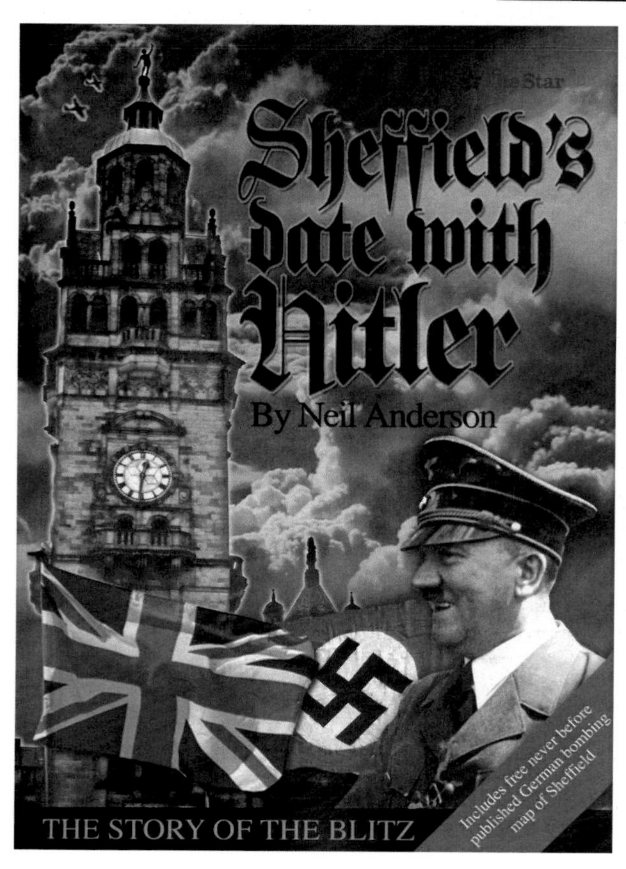
The Star
Sheffield's date with Hitler
By Neil Anderson
Includes free never before published German bombing map of Sheffield
THE STORY OF THE BLITZ

A WOMAN OF STEEL
RUBY- A DIAMOND FOREVER
BY STEPHEN JOHNSON
FOREWORD BY LORD MAYOR OF SHEFFIELD, COUNCILLOR SYLVIA DUNKLEY

The story of the city's
WOMEN OF STEEL
COMMEMORATING THE 70TH ANNIVERSARY OF THE SHEFFIELD BLITZ
INCLUDES ADDITIONAL RARE FOOTAGE OF KING GEORGE VI AND QUEEN ELIZABETH TOURING THE BOMBED OUT CITY IN DECEMBER 1940
The Star

BOMBS OVER
BRAMALL LANE
GROWING UP IN 1940s SHEFFIELD
BY KEN LEARY
FOREWORD BY NEIL ANDERSON,
AUTHOR OF 'SHEFFIELD'S DATE WITH HITLER'

About the author

Neil Anderson's interest in Sheffield's involvement in both world wars started with childhood memories of time spent with his great grandad, Harold Hickson.
He was one of the first people to answer Kitchener's call and sign up for the Sheffield City Battalion in World War One.
The fighting force were part of one of the biggest military disasters in history - the Battle of the Somme in 1916.
Harold was one of just a handful of survivors that came back to Sheffield and could only look on in horror as the country counted down to war once again in 1939.
His daughter, Neil's grandma, Dorothy Glover, provided much first hand evidence of life in the Anderson Shelter for his *Sheffield's Date With Hitler* book before she died, aged 93, in September 2009.
Neil has written for titles spanning *The Independent* to the *Yorkshire Post* and was a *Sheffield Telegraph* columnist for over a decade.
He has now written ten books about Sheffield and its history.
When he's not writing books he's busy running a successful media relations company (www.allcreditmedia.com) and publishing books through ACM Retro (www.acmretro.com).

Acknowledgements

Sheffield Newspapers for use of pictures, Sheffield Local Studies Library, Edward J. Mullins and his excellent History of Sheffield Fire Brigade (www.sfbhistory.org.uk) that were the source for much of Chapter 5, Dave Manvell, Terry Deary, Peter Stringfellow, Sandra Barley, Marlene Dale (nee Cavell), Lillian Clay, Maurice Wilkinson, Roy Shenton, Doreen Beeley, Doug Lightening, Haydn Anderson, Nellie Bennett, Joy Newton, Douglas Oldfield, Betty Ralph, Gerald Cartwright, Les Dinsdale, Marie Parkin, Emmie Gommersall (nee Pike), Jean Grindle and the staff and residents of Brackenfield Hall Care Home, Barry Baxter, George Turner, Marion Chapman, Peter Hallam, Mary Atkin, Betty Hudson, Shirley Smith, William Cooper, Greta Philips, Joyce Spurr, Sheila Pantry, Margaret Emery, Gladys Bunting (nee Couldwell), Gladys Garfitt, Teresa Oates, Betty Flanagan (nee Sheldon), Ray Mawhood, Pete Wood, Pat Wiles, Eddie Flanagan and Ben Ward

Dedicated to the memories of Harold Hickson and Dorothy Glover and the thousands of Sheffielders who lost their lives in WW1 and WW2.

All round inspiration:
Lowri, Ewan and Dylan Anderson

Transcriptions beyond the call of duty:
Lindsay McLaren

Sheffield Blitz Memorial Fund

Please help our cause

Forgotten Memories From A Forgotten Blitz is likely to be the last time we hear first hand from many of the contributors who are now well into their nineties.
The horror of what they went through is still as poignant today as it was in December 1940 and we have to thank them for agreeing to revisit those two hellish nights which saw many of them lose close friends and family.
We want to ensure future generations never forget what they went through - that's why we've set up the Sheffield Blitz Memorial Fund to ensure their memory, and the memory of thousands of people like them, live on.
Officially launched in November 2011, we are raising money to promote knowledge and education around the Sheffield Blitz and its devastating impact that changed the face of the city forever.
Our first aim is the creation of a Sheffield Blitz Memorial Trail with markers on key sites around the city centre. But we are hoping to do much more.
The campaign is backed by The Star, Sheffield City Council, Atkinsons, Moor Sheffield and Brassfounders.
Any donations would be gratefully received - however small.

Cheques should be made payable to the 'Sheffield Blitz Memorial Fund' and sent to:
ACM Retro, The Grange, Church Street, Dronfield, Sheffield S18 1QB.

Sheffield Blitz Memorial Fund bank account details:
Nat West account no. 52118665. Sort code 54-41-47

More information from us at: info@sheffieldblitz.co.uk

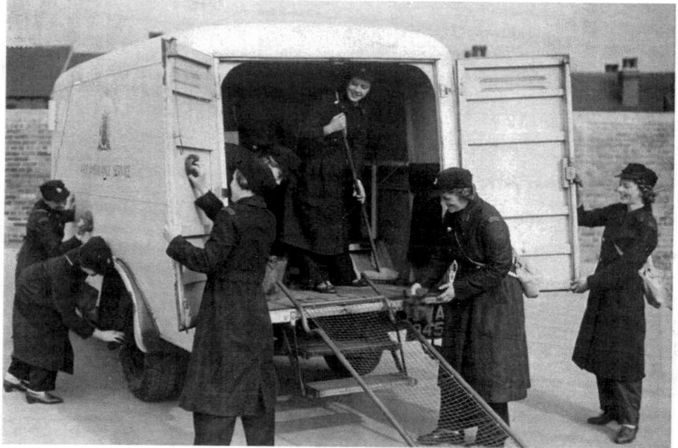